"Christians are a work in redemption, and not just wl show us the path to healing and restoration—and often, now that path guides us along so that we understand God's truth as it really is, especially when shared with compassion through the touch of a loved one, one like R.C. Jr.'s father. Theirs is an amazing story of a wise father and a searching son who both understand the power of Grace to change and heal. I highly recommend this wonderful book!"

—JONI EARECKSON TADA, FOUNDER AND CEO, JONI AND FRIENDS

"*Growing Up (With) R. C.* is an honest and insightful book. The love that R.C. Jr. has for his father emanates on every page. R.C. lifts the curtain, so to speak, to share some personal and powerful lessons he learned from his father. As the son of an influential Christian leader, I resonate deeply with his desire to honor his father, but also to share 'insider' stories and truths the world may not know. Like the experience of R.C. Jr., my dad was always engaging me in conversation to help me learn to think theologically about all areas of life. There were many times reading the book that I laughed out loud and thought, 'He's describing my dad!' I hope this book gets the wide readership it deserves."

—SEAN MCDOWELL, PHD, SPEAKER, PROFESSOR AT TALBOT SCHOOL OF THEOLOGY, AND AUTHOR OF MORE THAN EIGHTEEN BOOKS

"R.C. Jr. has long been my friend and yokefellow. His father has long been my mentor and hero. Reading the story of their lives together made me laugh and cry, rejoice and repent. Somehow, R.C. Jr. writes with an exceedingly rare combination of Gospel humility and Gospel boldness. This book is not to be missed. *Coram Deo!*"

—DR. GEORGE GRANT, PASTOR AND AUTHOR

GROWING UP

(With)

R. C.

*Truths I Learned About Grace,
Redemption, and the Holiness of God*

R. C. Sproul Jr.

Ichthus Publications · Apollo, Pennsylvania

Copyright © 2019 by R. C. Sproul Jr.

All rights reserved. No part of this publication may be reproduced, stored in a retrieval system, or transmitted, in any form or by any means, electronic, mechanical, photocopying, recording or otherwise, without prior permission of the publisher or the Copyright Licensing Agency.

Our goal is to provide high-quality, thought-provoking books that foster encouragement and spiritual growth. For more information regarding Ichthus Publications, other IP books, or bulk purchases, visit us online or write to support@ichthuspublications.com.

Unless otherwise indicated, all Scripture quotations are from the ESV® Bible (The Holy Bible, English Standard Version®), copyright © 2001 by Crossway, a publishing ministry of Good News Publishers. Used by permission. All rights reserved.

Scripture marked KJV taken from the King James Version, public domain.

Printed in the United States of America.

Cover image licensed by Shutterstock.

Growing Up (With) R.C.
Truths I Learned About Grace, Redemption, and the Holiness of God
ISBN: 978-1-946971-49-4 (paperback)
ISBN: 978-1-946971-50-0 (ebook)

www.ichthuspublications.com

Contents

Foreword by Tullian Tchividjian vii
Introduction xi

1. Becoming R. C. 1
2. Growing Bigger Eyes 9
3. Cosmic Treason 17
4. Temperature's Rising 25
5. Patriarchal Principle #1 33
6. Looking for Wisdom in All the Wrong Places 41
7. Beyond Freedom and Dignity 49
8. My Hometown 57
9. Dreaded Locks 65
10. My Droogs 73
11. Whatcha Got? 81
12. Santini! 89
13. Angels Dancing on My Pinhead 97
14. Those Angry Young Men and Their Haughty
    Cacophonies 105

15. Mice on the Doorstep 113

16. Treasure Without a Map 121

17. Not a Piece of Chalk 129

18. "As Is" 137

19. Now Is the Time 145

20. Honor Your Father 153

21. He Is My Friend 161

22. Great 169

23. Two Words 177

24. Me and My Shadow 185

25. The Good Fight 193

Afterword by Lisa C. Sproul 201

Foreword

In his book titled *The Autobiography and Deliverance of Mark Rutherford*, William Hale White describes Mr. Rutherford's childhood pastor, Brother Holderness, and his willingness to confess publically that he was a sinner, a broken man just like everybody else. White writes that Holderness would openly "confess sins" which, while many, "were never given in any detail which would have made his confession of some value." He never prayed without "telling all of us that there was no health in him, and that his soul was a mass of putrefying sores, and everybody thought the better of him for his self-humiliation." But, White says, if the pastor would have confessed one actual indiscretion, he "would have been visited by suspension or expulsion."[1]

White makes a profound point: It is one thing to confess that you're a sinner; it is another thing altogether to confess your sins. I have observed that people love it when preachers or Christian leaders say they are fallen just like the rest of us, until that preacher or Christian leader does something that the rest of us fallen people do. When that happens, the love and admiration quickly turn to disgust, disillusionment, and, all too often, social expulsion.

Growing up in a Christian environment, I was taught from an early age the importance of truth. I was reminded again and again in different ways by many people how important it is to tell the truth, that God's Word is truth, that Jesus is the truth, and that the truth will set you free. I'm eternally grateful for that. We are lost without the absolute anchoring of truth. But one aspect of the truth that I can't recall hearing about is the need to tell the truth, the whole truth, and nothing but the truth about ourselves.

The fact is, however, that no one will pay any lasting attention to all of our talk about the importance of truth unless we demonstrate our own belief in truth by first telling the truth about ourselves—the ugly, hard truth that we desperately don't want anyone to know. And this is the primary thing I appreciate about R. C.'s book.

It's a memoir of sorts, with the specific intent of reflecting on what it was like to have a famous theologian for a father—a theologian I deeply admired. And the picture he paints is of a man who loved his son through all of his son's ups and downs—a picture that reflects the way God loves us. But it's R. C.'s willingness to talk about his ups and downs—specifically his downs—that made the biggest impact on me.

Refusing to present a Photoshopped version of himself, he discusses his life as it really is. He not only confesses that he is a sinner, but he confesses his sins. Like the rest of us, R. C. is a broken, fallen human. But he's not content simply sharing that fact generically; he specifies the ways in which he has fallen. It takes a robust, God-given belief in the truth of the Gospel—a Gospel his father taught him—to embrace and confess the truth about yourself in a way that risks rejection. And R. C. doesn't hesitate in doing just this.

In Psalm 51, following his adulterous relationship with Bathsheba and the subsequent murder of her husband, Uriah, King David breaks down. He loses his composure as he composes his song of confession. He comes clean. He admits his sin, acknowledges his need for

Foreword

forgiveness, and appeals to God's mercy. He petitions for God's unfailing love in the wake of his greatest failure. Keenly aware of his transgressions and unable to shake his shame, he begs for God's compassionate cleansing. He knows that God and God alone can remove his guilt, set him straight, renew him, restore him, and sustain him. He knows that while others may never forgive him, he will be okay as long as he can be assured of God's forgiveness.

Having pleaded to God for these things, David makes God a promise:

> Then I will teach transgressors your ways,
> and sinners will return to you.
> Deliver me from bloodguiltiness, O God,
> O God of my salvation,
> and my tongue will sing aloud of your righteousness.
> O Lord, open my lips,
> and my mouth will declare your praise
> (Psalm 51:13–15).

He promises God that he will steward his failures in service to God and others. He promises God that he will tell the world about the seriousness of sin and the gloriousness of grace. He promises God that he will spend the rest of his days singing of His righteousness and declaring His praiseworthiness. This man after God's own heart vows to sing about the heart of God from a place of deep experience that he could not have known apart from failure.

This is what R. C. does—he sings about the heart of God.

It might be tempting to miss the primary tune of this book and see it simply as a sweet melody about the more personal side of a famous man composed by a deeply appreciative and adoring son. But this book has a louder song to sing. It's ultimately a composition about the God who meets our guilt with His grace, our sin with His salvation, our faults with His forgiveness, and our perversion with His purity; the God of repeat-offenders who irrevocably clothes us in a suit of righteousness.

I've said elsewhere that every person I have ever known who has crashed and burned, and as a result, come to terms with their own powerlessness, has taught me something about God's love and grace and forgiveness that I would've never known otherwise. This includes R. C.

Thank you, my friend, for reminding me that while my sin reaches far, God's grace reaches farther.

Tullian Tchividjian

Introduction

My head hung in shame as I shuffled my feet toward the jury box, chained and shackled along with the other accused men. As I stood in an Indiana courtroom, I did so not as a juror but as a prisoner. I would much rather report that my imprisonment was unjustly initiated for protesting the ongoings at an abortion mill or for publicly proclaiming the gospel in violation of a city ordinance. But such was not the case. Instead the reason was far more disturbing.

Despite the fog of confusion about the day's preceding events, I knew where I was and, tragically, why I was there. The intervening hours, however—the ones that lay between emptying that bottle and emerging from inebriation in the "drunk tank"—remained empty. I had no memory of them, but I was sensible enough to be haunted by my actions as I recalled them. My shame was twofold: Not only had I driven drunk, but I had done so with my two sons in the car, putting them in potential danger.

Overcoming whatever sense of shame I felt at the moment, I raised my head slowly in fear, unsettled by what might be. I now wanted answers to two important questions: *Were my boys okay?* And, *Did my new bride still love me?* As I looked around the courtroom, my eyes met my wife, appearing dignified and beautiful. She mouthed two compelling sentences: "The boys are okay. I love you." My fears were gone. My shame, however, remained.

When my turn came before the court, I stood and gave my opening plea—not guilty. Was that a lie? I knew what I had done, but I didn't yet know all that it would mean.

I was led out of the courtroom, still in chains, and back to the holding cell. There, surrounded by lawbreakers just like me, my fears returned. What extraordinary burdens had I just laid on my bride? What was she doing at the present? Would she be okay? Would I be safe inside here? How long would I be here? How exactly would this impact the future?

To make matters worse, my wife and I had been together so briefly, and with the magic of smartphones, I didn't even know her phone number to reach her in the event that I had the opportunity. She loved me. That much I knew; she had told me so. But I didn't know exactly what to do in that moment, how to help her wade through this newfound mess that I had foisted upon our family.

Thoughts of what I'd done flashed through my mind and left me with a sense of disquiet. My stomach churned as I reflected on my actions—after all, what else did I have to do just sitting there, waiting?—and I arrived at a more raw, existential awareness of my sins and weaknesses. Minutes passed into hours, and the disconcerting recollections playing over and over in my mind left me restless, sickened. I didn't even have the stomach to eat a meal, a bologna sandwich, so I passed. Instead I studied the men around me, not joining in with them, but taking in their conversations.

And I prayed. My shame weighed me down, pinning me to the cold concrete bench in that overcrowded ten-by-ten cell. I knew the future looked bleak, yet I knew enough in that moment to ask my Lord to forgive me. The past, the night before, remained—as it still remains—beyond my reach, yet I knew enough to ask Him to comfort me with His certain promises.

My mind raced to the coming revelations. It struck me that my downfall would probably surprise few. I had already had scandal in my life. None, however, could be summed up by a breathalyzer test, a police report, and the dutiful, graphically-detailed recounting of my case on the World Wide Web. I drew some small comfort in knowing that what others would learn about me was no more and no less than what I already knew about myself: I was objectively guilty.

Despite having logged many hours through the years watching and reading crime dramas, I wasn't prepared for that surreal moment. I didn't know what else to expect. My phone, my wallet, even my watch and wedding band had been confiscated at booking. All I could do was hope and wait as, one by one, my fellow inmates were led away, either to the general population of the jail or, having made bail, to the general public. I gave thanks that I had been kept safe, that the police had treated us all with an aloof dignity.

As I watched others being brought in, booked, fingerprinted, having their mug shots taken, I acquired a sense of the process I had been through the night before. The shame doubled down, not only because I had been through that process but because I had no memory of it.

Nearly twenty-four hours after first being detained, I was led out of the jail and to my waiting bride. The relief, the precipitous drop in adrenaline, called forth a torrent of tears as she held me and as I held her, my mouth blubbering inexpressible remorse and regret: "I'm so sorry. I love you. I'm so sorry."

My little boys were there as well, seemingly unfazed by the events. They too offered hugs and forgiveness as we made our way to the waiting car. I could not help but see that they were wearing their police badge stickers proudly, given to them while they had been looked after following my arrest.

The relief of my release, however, was quickly replaced with horror at the revelation of what I'd done. My wife gently but accurately recounted what she had experienced and what she had learned. The night before, she had called with a change in plans; rather than coming to pick up the boys and me and take us to dinner, she wondered if we could meet her at the restaurant. I agreed, but I never made good on my promise. She sat in the restaurant with her friend, waiting for us, her worry escalating. *Where is he? He's only fifteen minutes away, and it's been nearly an hour.*

When she tried calling me, I didn't answer. And then her phone rang. Only it wasn't me calling; it was the police. They asked if she knew who was driving her car. After she told them I was driving her car, they asked her if there was any reason I might be impaired. The only thing my wife could think of at that moment was my blood pressure issues. The possibility of intoxication never even entered her mind. After all, she didn't keep alcohol in the house.

Yet there I was, driving thirty miles per hour on the interstate with a blowout—sirens blaring behind me, lights flashing—and I just kept going, seemingly oblivious to my surroundings. Whatever eventually compelled me to pull off the road—instinct perhaps?—came as a welcome relief, not only to the police following me but also to my young passengers. My boys were stricken with terror, crying, afraid the police might fire their weapons at us to get me to stop.

After I finally came to a stop, emerged from the vehicle, and failed my sobriety test, the police called my wife back, giving her instructions on where to pick up our boys and letting her know I would be spending the night in jail. That night was the first time she learned that I had been drinking. She brought the boys home, put them to bed, and set about the business of praying, worrying, and

Introduction

alerting my extended family. She had less sleep that night than I did, scrolling through my text messages, exploring my social media sites, trying to find a rational explanation as to why I had consumed so much alcohol.

There is, of course, no explanation. Excuses are just that—excuses. Even to pin the crime on my sin nature would be a kind of deflection, as if my wickedness could excuse my wickedness. I drank too much because I chose to drink too much. I put my boys in the back seat because I chose to put them in the back seat. I put the key in the ignition because I chose to put the key in the ignition. And there is no time machine that can take me back to choose again. I sowed the wind and blew into that breathalyzer the whirlwind.

That's what I did. I'm not the only one to have made such foolish, sinful decisions. Nor am I the only one to have their sins covered by the press. Usually, however, when someone's DUI makes the news, that somebody is a celebrity: an athlete, a politician, an actor. It is not often that the son of a well-respected theologian—and who himself professes faith and has been blessed to teach and preach—gets into that kind of trouble.

So what do we do? I believe the answer to that question, no matter what circumstances we find ourselves in, is as simple as it is clear: Repent and believe the gospel. By God's grace, that's just what I did. Not, of course, for the first time. And therein lies the challenge—acknowledging that repentance and belief must be ongoing.

Believers become believers in just that fashion, by repenting and believing the gospel. We affirm, most of us, that even after we repent, we continue to struggle with sin. What we expect and hope, however, is that those sins will be smallish sins, peccadilloes, nothing scandalous. We hope and expect such because we pay insufficient attention to the Word of God. Noah, Abraham, Jacob, Moses,

David, Solomon, Hezekiah, and Peter all fell flat in a big way—*after* coming to faith.

The Lord was at work in each of them. Just as He was at work in me. It is true that we grow more like Jesus every day. And it is true that we all still sin in scandalous ways. Perhaps no sin ever committed, however, was as shocking as that committed by our first parents. They had everything and willfully threw it all away.

I don't say this to minimize my actions or to excuse them. Far from it. In fact, one could argue that I had *even more* than Adam and Eve. True, I was born with a sin nature, and true, I was raised by a pair of sinners. But even with that, I know that I have been blessed from birth.

I was raised by parents who loved me well, loved each other well, and best of all, loved Jesus well and taught me about Him from infancy. In my father, I had an example of a godly man before my eyes my whole life. I had, as well, every material advantage; I never went to bed hungry, never worried about where my next meal would come from.

I was given the finest education imaginable, both of my parents making sacrifices to make that possible. I sat at the feet of the greatest theologians of our day—listening to them from pews, in classrooms, and even around the dinner table. I was raised in faithful, God-fearing churches, and I professed faith at a young age. One could argue that my upbringing was nearly Edenic.

Yet I still manage to sin, to sin regularly, and to sin outrageously. I am as dependent on His grace, on the finished work of Christ, as was the thief on the cross.

There are differences between Adam and Eve and me. They were not indwelt by the Holy Spirit; I am. They were not already rescued from His judgment; I have been. They did not have the complete Word of God; I do. They did not have the examples of those who had gone before them and fell into sin, nor did they have the example of the one Man who was tempted in every way yet never sinned; I do. In many ways, I have it easier than Adam and Eve, as I am living on this side of the cross.

Grace, though, is still necessary in my life. I, who have been given so much by my heavenly Father, too often have squandered what He's lavished on me. I have wasted the gifts He's given me, grumbled in the midst of the blessings He's showered upon me. And I have done all of this not just on this side of the cross but on this side of *my coming* to the cross. I—who have already known His grace and forgiveness, who have already been convicted of my sins—still run headlong back into my sins.

It is discouraging. And it's no wonder that when I fall, the devil is right by my side whispering in my ear, casting doubt in my mind concerning the promises of God. He is there to remind me that I am not worthy of grace, that I do not deserve it, that I am nothing but an abject failure.

The strange thing is that he's absolutely right. It is often said that an effective lie must contain an element of truth to be believed, and this one is nothing but the truth: I am an abject failure who doesn't deserve grace. The lie, in this case, is found in what isn't spoken—the false notion that because I do not deserve grace, that because I am a failure, I will not receive grace. The truth is, when I receive grace, it is precisely because I *am* a failure who doesn't deserve it.

You see, grace itself, at its very core, is scandalous. Of course I don't deserve it—that's what makes it grace. The right response to the devil's accusations is not to deny the truth but to deny the lie. Martin Luther, no stranger to the accusations of the devil, had it right when he said,

> So when the devil throws your sins in your face and declares that you deserve death and hell, tell him this: "I admit that I deserve death and hell, what of it? For I know One who suffered and made satisfaction on my behalf. His name is Jesus Christ, Son of God, and where He is there I shall be also!"[2]

God's grace, however, is not merely enough to forgive me; it is enough to heal me. God doesn't accept me just the way I am; He accepts me just the way His Son is. And even more amazing, He has promised to make me like His Son. We are told, "If we confess our sins, He is faithful and just to forgive us our sins and to cleanse us from all unrighteousness" (1 John 1:9).

Note that this promise begins when we confess our sins. Defending ourselves, excusing ourselves, is the opposite of confessing our sins. When we acknowledge our sins, when we own them for what they are, then He will forgive us. And in doing so, according to this verse, God will be just.

How is that justice? Isn't that the opposite of justice? I'm guilty after all. But it *is* justice, because of Christ's work on the cross. He was declared guilty in my place. He took the judgment that was due to me. The debt has not been merely written off, but paid, in full, for all my sins.

Does this then mean that I can sin all I like? Since He's declared me innocent, can I go on sinning? No, because the promise in 1 John 1:9 isn't just forgiveness, but cleansing. He is cleansing me from all unrighteousness. I do not receive grace because I am getting better; rather, I am getting better because I am receiving grace.

It is He who works in me both to do and to will His good pleasure (Philippians 2:13). Of course I still sin. In fact, immediately after affirming God's promise to forgive and to cleanse us, John adds, "If we say that we have not sinned, we make Him a liar, and His word is not in us" (1 John 1:10). But He is at work. The same power that called all creation into being, the same power that raised Jesus from the dead, is at work, even in a scandalous sinner like me.

I carry with me two names. I am R. C. Sproul Jr., the son of R. C. Sproul. More importantly, I am a Christian, a younger brother of the Son of God. I have two fathers. I brought shame on them both. I am comforted, however, to know that my elder Brother took my shame on Himself. I have wept over my sin. I have confessed it to those in authority over me. And because of God's grace, I have been forgiven. The only One who matters remembers my sin no more. Having repented and believed the gospel, what do I do now? Repent, believe the gospel, and proclaim the gospel that saves a wretch like me.

In the loss of my reputation, as with the loss of my father, I mourn. But on both accounts, I do not mourn as those who are without hope. The gospel of Jesus Christ moves me from mourning to dancing—dancing like King David with joy before the Lord with all his might (2 Samuel 6:14).

1

Being R. C.

Though I was there for it all, I have no memory of it. It was, however, a red-letter day, in more ways than one. It was July 1, 1965, the day I was born, and I suspect I will never live through a more traumatic day. My mother was going through the agony of giving birth, and I, the agony of being born. My father, I suspect, was pacing the waiting room at St. Francis Medical Center in Pittsburgh, the smoke spewing out of him, a mirror of the belching steel mills along the three rivers.

My parents had planned to name me Steven Audent Sproul. I don't know for sure what prompted that, but if I had to guess, Steven was probably for the New Testament's first martyr. Audent is a Latin word that means, roughly, "One who dares." My father, however, didn't dare. That is, while my mother was in the hospital recovering from giving birth, my father also had an aunt who was dying in that same hospital. He went to visit her, gave her the good news, and she took the occasion to make as her dying wish that my father continue the family tradition and name me "Robert C."

My father was the third generation in a row to follow this pattern—his father had named him Robert Charles. My grandfather had been Robert C, with no middle name (like Ike). His father before him had been Robert Cecil. Thus, I was named Robert Craig. And my great aunt went to her grave a satisfied woman.

My birth, however, was not the only excitement that day. My father's father had died while my father was still in high school. His mother had bravely finished the job of raising her only son while cherishing two deep goals: She wanted to have a grandson born to carry on the family name, and she wanted to see her son ordained to gospel ministry. The day the stork delivered me to my mother, the mailman delivered to my grandmother two tokens of her second goal—an invitation to my father's ordination service and the dress she had ordered to wear for that event.

On the morning of July 2, my sister Sherrie, all of three years old and giddy with delight over my birth, went into our grandmother's bedroom to wake her for the day. Our grandmother, however, either overwhelmed with excitement or drifting in contentment, had awakened in Paradise sometime during the night. The lifeless shell of her body refused to respond to my sister. My father had gained a son and lost a mother in the same 24 hours. "The Lord giveth, and the Lord taketh away" was made real to him on that day. She was buried in the dress she had ordered for my father's ordination.

From that day forward, my father faithfully poured his life into me. His method, which was profoundly biblical, was the very antithesis of flashy. Some years ago I published a book on homeschooling, entitled *When You Rise Up*. That brief work was mostly an exposition of the principles found in Deuteronomy 6, wherein Moses, inspired by the Holy Spirit, enjoins God's people:

> Hear, O Israel: The LORD our God, the LORD is one! You shall love the LORD your God with all your heart, with all your soul, and with all your strength. And these

words which I command you today shall be in your heart. You shall teach them diligently to your children, and shall talk of them when you sit in your house, when you walk by the way, when you lie down, and when you rise up. You shall bind them as a sign on your hand, and they shall be as frontlets between your eyes. You shall write them on the doorposts of your house and on your gates (verses 4–9).

I laid out in that book three principal points: the message, the method, and the means. God here commands His people to speak to their children of the things of God. They are to tell their children who God is, what God has done, what God requires, and what God has promised. That is the message.

The method is simple and organic. Parents are to speak with their children and to do so in the context of life. "When you sit in your house" does not exclude when you sit in your fields. "When you walk by the way" does not exclude when you go for your morning jog. "When you lie down, and when you rise up" does not exclude any of the hours in between. The pedagogy is an antipedagogy. Just talk to your kids.

The means is as simple as the method. God here calls parents to do the job. He does not command Israel to hire professionally trained tutors or highbrow scholars. It's the job of the parents.

Although I was not homeschooled as a child, my parents took this command to heart. We learned not by following someone else's curriculum but by talking. And we talked not by scheduling time to talk but simply by talking in the ebb and flow of our days.

I did not so much learn from my father as absorb him. One of the blessings of organic learning is that it does not just encourage the learning of propositions but it trains the mind in how those propositions relate. The harmonizing of information, the unifying of the diversity, is as important as the disparate bits of truth themselves. Let me illustrate with a story.

I was still in high school and was speaking—or should I say debating?—with the man who then discipled me. We embraced the same theological system, the very one my father had taught me. But on matters of apologetics, we differed. I aligned myself with my dad's view, which was out of the mainstream in our circles. My teacher was trying to win me over to his point of view on apologetics, and he explained to me that we all believe what we believe because someone in authority tells us what to believe.

"You believe that a ball is a ball," he said, "because when you were a baby, your father showed you a ball and said 'ball.'"

I knew that all I needed was one counterexample to destroy his argument. And one came immediately to mind, a theological issue on which my mentor and I agreed and with which my father disagreed: infralapsarianism versus supralapsarianism. Simply put, this is the understanding of *when* God ordained the salvation of His people.

"If that's so," I said, "then how come my dad is an infralapsarian and I am a supralapsarian?"

My mentor didn't skip a beat but just smiled down at me and said, "Because your father taught you to be logical."

He did do that. I remember him giving me logic exercises in junior high school. I remember, not long after that, sitting in my bedroom listening to cassettes of a six-part lecture series he had prepared on logic. This will not surprise those who are familiar with my father's teachings over the years; he was known for the laser precision of his reasoning.

While his book *The Holiness of God* was perhaps the most widely read, it is likely that his *Chosen By God* had an even greater impact. Untold thousands came to embrace the sovereignty of God over our salvation by reading that book and by coming along for the ride as my father relentlessly pursued that vexing question of how God's freedom and our freedom relate.

The trouble is this: We tend to equate careful, logical thought with a corresponding coldness of heart. Those who knew my father only from a distance could understandably have jumped to the wrong conclusion about him and presumed him cold. My father's heart, however, was as warm as his mind was sharp. I learned from him more than simply sound theology. As my father modeled Jesus, I learned forgiveness, compassion, humor, loyalty, and love.

What follows then is not by any stretch a biography. That will be handled by far more competent hands than mine. Rather, what follows is more a remembrance, a looking back at the lessons I learned in the backyard, in the car, in the woods, and at the dining table.

I know I have been deeply and profoundly blessed to have R. C. Sproul for a father. As I like to remind people, however, the blessing wasn't because he was such a great theologian but because he was such a great father. And the best thing about him was that, because he knew how much he needed Jesus, he told me about Jesus. My father was not a perfect man, but every day of our lives together, he pointed me toward our perfect elder Brother. Which is why, when we laid my father's remains into the ground, these are the words I was privileged to speak:

> From an early age there was a call on his life. Though raised in what appeared to be a normal family, one swaddled in love, it was apparent early on that this one would be used mightily by God. He was, in a manner of speaking, pushed into gospel ministry, both by his heavenly Father and by his earthly mother. While he

was still a young man, his labors in God's vineyard were blessed. He spoke as one with authority, and before long, crowds began to gather. Like David versus Goliath, he went into battle with theological liberals and stood firm on the Word of God, on the promises of God.

Crowds began to flock to him as he travelled around his home country, though from time to time those crowds would wax and wane. When he gave the people what they wanted, the crowds grew. When, however, he spoke of the sovereignty of God, the crowds tended to shrink. This man was deeply loved by a select few who knew him intimately, apart from his public ministry, the man in private. Too often, however, even they let him down.

I'm speaking, of course, of the man we have gathered here today to honor, Jesus Christ of Nazareth. For surely we would dishonor R. C. Sproul were we to gather to honor R. C. Sproul.

There are myriad ways to describe my father's life mission—to awaken as many people as possible to the holiness of God in all its fullness; to show people the character of God; to defend the faith once delivered. The best description, however, is the simplest: He lived to tell people about Jesus.

We would be wise to remember that the serpent is more crafty than any of the beasts of the field. He is able to take the most humbling of truths and turn them, in us, into an occasion for pride. R. C. Sproul had the intellectual firepower to describe with precision that biblical gospel. He had the communications gifting to reach millions with the message. He possessed the moral fortitude to stand strong in defense of the gospel. And God blessed his reach, his impact.

As we lower this body into the ground, however, we must embrace, to our core, that R. C. Sproul, like each of us, was a sinner saved by grace, justly deserving God's displeasure. His greatest success was in recognizing his failure, that he fell short. His most heroic act was to rest in the Hero. We do not, in taking this occasion to remember this truth, dishonor the man, but honor the message. More important still, we honor the meaning of the message, Jesus, the Savior of sinners.

The scope of his ministry, the love of his family and friends, the respect of his peers—these were not where my father found his comfort. Rather, his only comfort, in life and in death, is that he belongs to his faithful Savior, Jesus Christ, who at the cost of His own blood, has fully paid for all our sins and has completely freed us from the dominion of the devil; that He protects us so well that, without the will of our Father in heaven, not a hair can fall from our heads. Indeed, that everything must fit His purpose for our salvation. Therefore, by His Holy Spirit, He also assures us of eternal life, making us wholeheartedly willing and ready to live, and to die, for Him.

Therefore, as we commit these earthly remains to the ground, we do so with confidence. We do not bury the body, but plant it, knowing it will blossom in perfection when the Perfect comes.

The Apostle Paul wrote to the church at Thessalonica: "Brothers, we do not want you to be ignorant about those who fall asleep, or to grieve like the rest of men, who have no hope. We believe that Jesus died and rose again and so we believe that God will bring with Jesus those who have fallen asleep in Him. According to the Lord's own word, we tell you that we who are still alive, who are left till the coming of the Lord, will not precede those who have fallen asleep. For the Lord Himself will come down from heaven, with a loud command, with the voice of the archangel and with the trumpet call of God, and the dead in Christ will rise first. After that, we who are still and live and left will be caught up together with them in the clouds to meet the Lord in the air. And so we will be with the Lord forever. Therefore, encourage each other with these words" (1 Thessalonians 4:13–18).

Christ has died. Christ is risen. Christ will come again.

And the just shall live by faith.

2

Growing Bigger Eyes

Most of you came to "know" my father through either something you read or something you heard. When you think of him, you think of teaching, or preaching, or writing. I, however, knew him before I knew the first thing about theology or the Bible. My earliest memory of him was the sight of him leaping. It wasn't, however, for joy.

I must have been all of three years old. I survived the sixties, not hitting the haze of teenage rebellion, but living through the recklessness of the age. We did not wear helmets when riding our bicycles. Our car seats were little more than metal contraptions designed mostly to hold us down, not to keep us safe. Parents generally didn't worry about such things back then.

That may explain how I came to be sitting in the front seat of the family car, alone, while it was running. I'm not sure where the rest of the family was—my attention was captured by the various nobs and buttons. I managed, somehow, to pull a lever, moving the car from park into reverse.

As the car began to glide down our driveway, I jumped into the back seat, more out of fear than out of an attempt to hide my guilt.

Peering over the front seat, I saw the front screen door of our house tear open and my dad run across the narrow porch before hurdling over the hedge, across the yard, and into the driver's seat. He applied the brakes, returned us safely to park, and all was right with the world, the car's tail just barely inched onto our suburban street.

That first memory captures what I first saw in my father. To me, he was a superhero. His role, like Batman watching over Gotham, was to keep us all safe.

It was not unusual for my mother and me to wake each morning before my father. After I had consumed my sugar-coated, sugar bomb cereal, she would send me into their bedroom to wake him. It was a liturgy of sorts, as I would stand by the side of the bed, gently urging him, "Daddy, it's time to get up." He would rouse just a bit, pretend to be asleep, and then sweep me up into the bed and into his arms. My part of the liturgy was to try to wriggle away. I would push and pull, but there was no escape. He loved me, and he would never let me go.

As I grew older, my ability to appreciate my father grew with me. I was all of eight years old and just beginning to enter the wide world of sports. Football and baseball were my favorites, just as they were for every other boy in my era. It was not in the playing fields that I had my epiphany, however, but in the basement. There, I found an old footlocker. I opened it with all the zeal of a pirate opening a treasure chest. And I found treasure indeed.

The footlocker was filled to the brim with mementoes of my father's sports past. There were newspaper clippings, complete with photos, of him in high school, driving in the winning run. There were varsity letters from Clairton High School football, basketball, and baseball. There were trophies, pennants, and a baseball—a game ball, signed by his grateful teammates. (I confess that, while I knew these were all treasures, that baseball's utility one day outweighed its sentimental value. My friend and I lost our ball in the weeds, and so I ran home for a replacement: my dad's signed ball. It soon joined its cousin in the weeds.)

About this time, Ligonier Ministries started, then as the Ligonier Valley Study Center. It served as a sort of battlefield seminary, a place where parachurch workers could come and receive theological training. That training happened in our living room. It was common for me, as a little boy in my pajamas, to leave the confines of the den where I was watching television and cross that living room to fetch a bowl of cereal. And there would be scores, if not hundreds, of young men and women listening as my father lectured.

I did not yet have much of an appreciation for theology, but I was impressed that all these people came to listen to my father. Those same students often graced our dining room, sharing meals and conversation.

From time to time my father would loosen the mood at these dinners with a bit of comedy. He would put me on his lap, put his hand up the back of my shirt, and have me pretend to be (or demonstrate that I was) his "dummy."

He had already taught me a bit of philosophy. He would ask his dummy, "Who believed the world was made of water?"

And I would chirp, "Thales."

"Who believed the world was made of atoms?" he would ask.

"Democritus," I would reply.

The biggest laugh, however, came when he would ask me, "Who wrote the Bible?"

I would grin widely and proclaim, with all the gusto of a proud young boy, "You did, Daddy."

My theological ignorance was such that I did not know that my father, my hero, walked with theological giants. Visitors to the study center included such towering figures as Chuck Colson, the great apologist John Warwick Montgomery, John Gerstner, James Montgomery Boice, and J. I. Packer, just to name a few. And I do remember the buzz created when we received a visit from Francis Schaeffer. (What I remember most, though, were his knickers and long hair, leading me to wonder if we'd been visited by an elf.)

It was not until later, when I was in high school, that I added to my hero's resume that he was himself a theological giant. My own immersion in theology happened almost by accident, as two streams of providence flowed together. First, my father came to speak at the school I attended.

With few strong educational options close to home in southwest Pennsylvania, I had been sent to Wichita Collegiate School in Kansas, where I was awarded a "scholarship" to attend. All that was required was that my father come and speak for the school's "Spiritual Emphasis Week." Clearly the school, its faculty, and its students were not wholeheartedly committed to the Christian faith, with an event like "Spiritual Emphasis Week" on the calendar.

Despite the school's aloof relationship with Christianity, my father came to speak with both guns blazing. He determined to teach these students, K–12, about divine predestination. For three days he explored, explained, exposited—until the whole school was left agape in utter shock. Then he flew home, leaving me there to mop up. I learned theology not so I could defend the Bible, but so I could defend my father.

That same spring I saw my father teaching again, when I went with my parents to the Congress on the Bible in San Diego. It was quite an event, a cavalcade of theological stars. There I heard for the first time that "elf" from my youth, Francis Schaeffer. Harold Lindsell and Kenneth Kantzer were there too. But nothing prepared me for the intersection of two heroes.

My father and I were riding the elevator in the hotel where we were staying. And in stepped none other than Josh McDowell.

"Dad," I whispered with urgency, "that's Josh McDowell!"

"Would you like to meet him?" he asked. "Josh, I'd like you to meet my son."

"Hey R. C.," Josh McDowell said to my father. "Good to see you."

OH MY STARS. My dad's prestige lifted off like a Project Mercury rocket. He knew Josh McDowell!

I met the man with all the courage of a shrinking violet.

Later that day my father mentioned to me in passing, "Tomorrow you'll be having breakfast with Josh McDowell."

I tried to correct him, to let him know I had studied the program for the conference thoroughly and that, had there been a "Breakfast with Josh" event, I would have seen it.

"No," he said. "It's not an event. It's just breakfast. Just the two of you."

The next morning I sat across from this rock star as he spoke to me as if I mattered. He asked me about my interests, answered my questions, and over the course of an hour, invested himself in me. I'm ashamed to say that, as I got older, I came to see my Josh McDowell fanboy stage in the same way a grown woman might look back on her Donny Osmond crush (or, perhaps if you're a bit younger, her Justin Timberlake crush). Josh, however, wasn't through with me yet.

Fifteen years later I received an envelope at work, addressed to me. I opened it and found inside one of those paper freebie luggage tags you get at the airport ticket counter. Scrawled across the back were these words—"Prayed for you today. Josh." My infatuation, or "man-crush" if you prefer, was back on and has not waned since.

GROWING UP (WITH) R. C.

This, then, was my introduction into my father's world. I bought into his theology, all the way down to my totally-depraved toes. What I loved was the elegance of the theology, how it fit together like a Swiss watch, each piece designed perfectly to move the next piece. I became not just the son of a systematic theologian but an aspiring systematic theologian myself. Because my father had trained my mind, I always tracked with him, and I subsumed all that he believed. I took to reading my father's books, and when I had plowed through them all, I moved on to devouring his manuscripts as they were being written.

I wanted to champion the theology of my champion—to defend it, to teach it, to give it hands and feet. As I grew older, I came to not only grasp the extent of my father's reach but to realize it was still growing. That proved to be a profound blessing. As I began to understand the nature of his singular gifts, I was able to let go of the foolish notion that I could ever become what he was.

Over the years, as people, wanting to be sensitive to my feelings, have thanked me "for your work and for your father's work," I've given one of two responses. One, I point out that that's like the French thanking the Americans and the Lithuanians for driving out the Nazis. Sure, they both helped, but who is kidding whom? Or I reply, "My father and I are in the same line of work, sort of like how the Space Shuttle and a paper airplane are both manmade flying machines."

After a decade—or maybe three?—I, without losing any of my convictions, grew out of what is often humorously called "the cage stage": that time in a young man's life when his zeal for his theological system makes him an obnoxious lout. And then I came to my last stage of admiration for my father.

In the end I came to admire him as I think he would have wanted: not for his athletic prowess, nor for his keen theological mind, but for his grace. I watched as my father exhibited a gentle and forgiving spirit to others with whom I had no patience. Even beyond this, I came to need—and I received—that same forgiving spirit personally.

If that theological system my father and I embrace affirms anything about God, it is that He is sovereign. If it affirms anything about man, it is that we are sinners. Strangely, given that fact, those who embrace that system have a well-earned reputation among the broader evangelical church as being the most arrogant and prideful of all professing believers. We manage to take this deep awareness of the scope of man's sinfulness and turn it into a badge of our own goodness. For my father, however, this doctrine—indeed *all* doctrine—was not merely a proposition to be affirmed but a present reality that should drive us to repentance. He was a forgiving man, because he knew that he was a forgiven man.

He was, in turn, a humble man because he knew that every gift he had was given to him by His perfect, loving Father.

3

Cosmic Treason

It was more than four decades ago, but I still feel the weight of the guilt. I was in the first grade. I arrived at the dinner table, only to discover a horror. There it was, looking deceptively innocent in a little white bowl: stewed tomatoes.

I did my best to hide my dread. I slowly ate the rest of my meal, occasionally eyeing the bowl and hoping for a miracle. None came. But opportunity did. My parents had to excuse themselves briefly from the table, and off I went, melding together swiftness and care, taking the bowl into the bathroom and dumping the tomatoes in the trash. (I knew better than to put them in the kitchen trash since they would surely be discovered there.)

When my parents returned, they noticed my empty bowl and queried me—had I eaten my tomatoes?

"Yes," I told them, without so much as a twitch.

"You didn't just throw them away did you?"

"No," I replied, cool as a cucumber.

My temperature began to rise slowly as I noticed they didn't seem satisfied with my answers.

"You really must tell us the truth and not lie," they pressed on. "Did you eat your tomatoes?"

They had upped the ante, and I met their bet, indignantly insisting, "I'm not lying! I ate my tomatoes."

Then they went all in.

"God knows the truth. He sees everything. He is, and was, right here in this room. There is no escaping His eyes. One last time: Did you eat your tomatoes?"

I folded. And wept. I couldn't go on with the lie, knowing that the lie had far outpaced the original sin.

There is a lesson in there, a lesson far more significant than the simple moralisms of "always tell the truth" or "always eat your vegetables." The lesson is that sin is real. And ugly. And so are its consequences.

At the end of our conversation, I felt the weight of my sin. I was a little grade-school version of Christian, the heavy-laden pilgrim from *Pilgrim's Progress*. I felt shame. My parents loved me. My heavenly Father loved me. And I was a liar to them all. Sure, I had not robbed a bank. I had not committed murder. But I had sinned. And then sinned yet again to cover my sin.

Though he did not say so that evening at the table, my father has wisely written that any sin, large or small, is cosmic treason. Whether we are sneaking a cookie or tossing our veggies, plotting insurrection or selling state secrets—it is all a bold proclamation to our Maker, the living God, that *we* will rule rather than Him, that *we* are wiser and stronger than He is.

There I was, six years old, and trying to wrest the Almighty from His eternal throne.

Now, those who are not Christians may think I am making a mountain out of a molehill. They may find in my minor deception no sin at all. If, after all, there is no objective standard of right and wrong, and if it was not wrong *to me*, then it was not anything to bother about at all. Right? And, they may think, if God is so petty as to be offended by a little boy not wanting to eat his veggies, He must be a small God indeed.

In fact, Christians are often tempted to think this same way. We are not so bold as to deny that sin is real. Instead, we embrace the idea that it is no big deal, nothing to get all worked up about. We borrow from pop psychology, which tells us that guilty feelings are unhealthy, and worse: that those feelings are not the fruit of any objective guilt.

Our God is loving, tender, gracious, and, in the words of King David, slow to anger and abounding in lovingkindness. Our Maker does not have a short fuse. Surely He must wink at the childish little sins of a small boy, we reason. Yes, we assent, Jesus came to save sinners—but just the really bad kinds of sinners, right? Jesus came to rescue drug dealers and gang members and murderers from their just punishments. Surely the rest of us have nothing to fear.

Perhaps we don't articulate our thoughts so boldly. We at least have enough shame to not say such things.

But we are fool enough to think them.

Unless, of course, we know who God is. Unless we remember that He is a consuming fire, that He is not a tame lion.

My father did not use the words "cosmic treason" at the dinner table that evening. He did, however, manage to communicate to my young, sinful mind the concept. Years later, the first time I heard him declare that "every sin is cosmic treason," it took me right back to those stewed tomatoes.

There are many speakers and writers who have a gift for superfluous rhetorical flourishes. The phenomenon is so common, in fact, that writing instructors have a phrase to describe it. They call it, "Look, Ma! I can write." It crops up whenever a writer would rather have his reader think about the writer than about what he is reading. Words, too often, outpace reality.

Such is not the case with "cosmic treason." If anything, words fall short of capturing the horror of even the smallest of sins. The measure of the wickedness of sin is found not in the grossness of the sin itself but in the glory of the One sinned against. It was bad enough that I had disobeyed the parents who had blessed me with life, who had nurtured and cared for me, who loved me. It was far worse that I had disobeyed the living and true God, the Creator and Sustainer of all things.

John Piper, for many years a friend and co-laborer of my father's and one of the theological giants whom I have been privileged to meet, captured well this truth about how my father spoke. He wrote, on the occasion of my father's passing:

> First, he had a serious and rigorous attention to the actual text of Scripture. He was not making his points in general, as his sermon floated in a fog above the text. He was reading the text. He was pushing my nose into the clauses. He was showing me what is really there. The shocking realities were real because they were really in the text.
>
> Second, over time, when you heard R. C. do this kind of thing repeatedly, you realized such serious and rigorous attention to the text was owing to his total devotion to the inerrancy and radical relevance of the Scriptures. He didn't believe that the message of biblical texts was innocuous and unexciting and therefore in need of artificial verbal boosters to make the thunder crack. Oh no. If you take the text seriously, and you realize this is the very word of God, you may expect that

its relevance will be repeatedly shocking.

Third, therefore, the jolting formulations of biblical truth that were sprinkled so liberally through R. C.'s preaching and writing were not artificially concocted to add effect, but strategically chosen to express reality. And he would say that the jolting expressions, if anything, fall short of, rather than exaggerate, the reality of the text.

Fourth, emerging from the exegesis, and rising in my heart, was an unashamed allegiance to the absolute sovereignty of God to show mercy or to judge according to His infinite wisdom. This was R. C.'s goal: a heart that is stunned and humbled and captivated by the transcendent greatness and purity of God.[3]

How often do we allow ourselves, as we study the character of God, to turn God into a mere object of study? Our thinking can easily become so abstract that we make of God Himself an abstraction. Aristotle called God "the unmoved mover." We may color in a few more lines than this, but as long as we have Him under our microscope, no matter how powerful it may be, we will miss that He is—that He not only exists, that He not only is transcendent and lifted up, but that He is immanent and near.

We are prone to seeing faith along a single axis. We believe, we affirm, what we know to be true—and seeking to grow, we add more information. We read and listen and study and dig deeper into the intricacies of the character of God. That's not a good thing; it's a *great* thing. There is, of course, nothing grander, nothing more sublime, that we could ever inquire about.

The problem is that sometimes we are so eager to believe more information that we forget the critical importance of believing more, down to our toes, the information that we already have. We are content to affirm that man is totally depraved, that sin infects every area of our being, that apart from His grace we can do nothing that is, strictly speaking, good. We are resistant, however, to let that truth hit home in all its soul-crushing power: I am a sinner. I was conceived in iniquity. I am a cosmic rebel.

A small view of God will birth a small view of sin. A small view of sin will birth a small view of the gospel. A small view of the gospel will shrink further still our view of God. It is not, after all, the knowledge of God that is the beginning of wisdom, but rather the fear of God (Proverbs 1:7). Any knowledge of God that does not drive us to our knees is counterfeit, a reflection of the knowledge that the devil himself has of God. He knows well who God is—and hates Him.

My father did not grasp, teach, proclaim, and defend the grandeur and holiness of God because he was smarter than other men. It was not because he had discovered some lost ancient text with a better explanation. He knew the holiness of God because he *knew* God and *feared* Him. And in his grace—and by *His* grace—my father taught me the same.

After I had wept over my sin with the tomatoes and over the sin of my lie in covering it up, I did not suddenly become mature. I was still a little boy with an immature understanding of God. But that seed had been planted in me, and over the years, that seed continued to be cultivated and nurtured by my parents. They were never heavy-handed towards us. They did not have hair-trigger temperaments, but were, like their heavenly Father, slow to anger and abounding in lovingkindness.

Out of that lovingkindness, however, they spoke the truth about the three great questions every human must wrestle with: (1) Who is God? (2) Who am I? (3) And how do I relate to God?

The answers? (1) God is holy. (2) I am not. (3) Apart from the work of Christ, His sacrificial death, and His vindicating resurrection, I would be rightly under God's wrath and judgment.

That lesson over stewed tomatoes did not magically transform me into a mature believer, nor did it end my life of sin and rebellion. What it did do, however, was forever remove from me the false notion that I was good. From that day forward, I knew I could never stand before the throne of God and protest my innocence on the basis of my ignorance. I knew what I was: a fool and a rebel, and without hope apart from Jesus.

I still won't eat stewed tomatoes . . . not because doing so might cause a traumatic flashback, but because they still smell and taste like old socks to me. Like the filthy rags I once kidded myself into believing my works of righteousness were.

On that day, my father figuratively stripped me naked, that I might run—not for the cover of fig leaves, but for the cover of the righteousness of Christ.

God is not a small god. Neither is He "too big" to take notice of our "petty" sins. Rather, He is too big to miss them—too big to wink at them or to brush them aside. Without the shedding of blood, the blood of the spotless Lamb, there is no remission of sins.

But worthy is the Lamb.

4

Temperature's Rising

Leonardo DaVinci is known around the world as a painter and a sculptor. He had prodigious gifts in both arenas. But his talent was not limited to those media. DaVinci was also an ardent student of the human body as well as an inventor. His skills were so broad-ranging that he truly was the prototypical "Renaissance man"—that is, a person possessing not just one great skill or even two great skills but possessing many varied skills, as well as the ability to interact with experts even outside of one's own areas of expertise.

My father is known around the world as a speaker and a writer. He had prodigious gifts in both arenas. But his talent was not limited to those media. My father was an insatiable procurer of new skills. He was, in a sense, a true Renaissance man.

His only trouble: He was as fickle about his interests as a teenager.

He followed a common pattern through the years. When he went into something new, he went all in. Whether it was painting, billiards, violin, astronomy, darts, archery, refinishing furniture, or building model trains, he began by reading everything he could find on the subject. His study would be littered with the best texts from the most proficient practitioners of whatever art he was seeking to acquire.

Next came the shopping spree. He would buy the top-of-the-line paintbrushes, pool cue, violin bow, or whatever accouterments went with the hobby. And not only would he acquire them all, but he would insist on procuring the best. He invariably had a coach along the way, a teacher who would unlock the mysteries of that field. And in the end, he would conquer whatever he had put his mind to—then put it away, so as to search for another mountain to climb.

There were, however, two great loves that never left his side: the piano and golf.

Few people are interested enough in the piano to put a grand piano in their living room. Fewer still put a baby grand into their own bedroom. My father, however, was among them.

Even within the realm of the piano, his interests were varied. I would hear bouncing from his bedroom boogie-woogie, followed by classical, followed by ragtime, followed by experimental jazz. We spoke often of the blessings of music, of aesthetics. He helped me grow past my teenage angst and to acquire a taste for more complex melodies than the simple chord progressions that had been my regular diet.

Golf, however, was likely an even deeper passion for him—and, I'm sorry to say, I probably almost ended his golf career before it had barely begun.

Wanting to include me in his passions, my father took me, for the first time, to Clovernook Country Club in Cincinnati, Ohio, when I was five. I sat in the passenger seat of the golf cart and watched as he took his first, then his second, practice swing. He took half a step forward, started his backswing, and just as the golf club began its downward arc, I cried out, "One more strike and you're out, Daddy!"

Fortunately for him, he fouled that one off.

As a boy, I did not have such varied interests. I had only one interest: sports. Whatever was in season, that's what I played, and

Temperature's Rising

that's what I watched. We were Pittsburghers, and thus we had a passion for the Pirates and for the Steelers.

In the providence of God, I was born at the right time, as my Pirates won the World Series when I was six. This was back when World Series games still were sometimes played during the day. I remember vividly how grateful I was when Miss Donchez, my first grade teacher (and my first crush), wheeled the television into the classroom one sunny October day so we could watch the game. The Pirates took the series again when I was fourteen, and in between, they often made the playoffs.

I started following the Steelers when I was seven, in 1972. Going back to their inaugural season of 1933, the Steelers had, up till that point, played in all of two playoff games—and won none. Thirty-nine whips of the lash. In fact, the Steelers had been so bad for so long that when they played in the first round of the playoffs that year, the stadium did not sell out, and thus the game wasn't even broadcast locally on television.

I remember vividly my father sitting at the kitchen table, listening to the game on a transistor radio. I spent most of that afternoon playing school with my older sister, constantly begging for recess breaks so I could check on the game. The last time I checked, my dad explained how dire the situation was.

"It's fourth and long, son," he said. "We're down, and there's only seconds left in the game."

He was preparing me to be disappointed. I, however, had the faith of a child.

"Don't worry, Dad," I said. "Franco will do something great, and the Raiders won't have any time to come back."

The very next play has been called the greatest play in the history of the NFL, carrying the moniker "The Immaculate Reception." Desperately avoiding a sack, Terry Bradshaw bobbed and weaved before hurling a pass toward "Frenchy" Fuqua. Jack Tatum, a Raider defensive back, hurtled toward Frenchy. The ball caromed off Tatum's shoulder and fell at the feet of Franco, who scooped it off his shoestrings and raced into the end zone to win the game.

This was the beginning of the greatest football dynasty ever. Two years later the Steelers won Super Bowl IX, then X, then XIII, then XIV—four championships in six years.

Just as I did not inherit my father's theological acumen, I did not inherit any of his athletic talent. I sought to make up for my lack of gifting with what I did have: fierce determination and knowledge of the game. I determined that, while I might often be outperformed on a given sporting field, I would never be outwilled or outsmarted—which, along with my red hair, ended up providing the perfect storm for outsized temper tantrums.

In the early days of the Ligonier Valley Study Center, we had a weekly ritual every summer. On Thursday evenings, staff, their families, students, and friends from around the community would gather for a hot dog roast. There were typically fifty or so people gathered, and after hot dogs, we would play a friendly game of softball. Kids were invited to play—but within certain parameters: When a kid came up to bat, only kids were allowed to field the ball.

As a kid, I loved these games . . . but I typically made only one at bat each game. Before my turn would come a second time, invariably I'd erupt.

It might be that a rule had been misapplied, and my sense of justice had been offended. The smiling little girl standing "safe" on first base, for instance, didn't temper my temper but rather aroused it. Clearly she had run out of the base path and should have been called out.

In the midst of this weekly ritual, my father and I had our own ritual. When I began to squeal and object, my father would simply point to our house. I'd been banished again, and even before my second at bat. He had no patience for my impatience, and I had no choice but to make that walk of shame all the way home.

It wasn't, however, just the rules that led to my tantrums. Often it was my own failures that prompted me.

A kid would be at bat and hit a simple pop-up, right to me. My heart would race, I'd open my glove, and too often, the ball would bounce right out. Then I would punish the glove for its failure, hurling it to the ground like I was spiking a football. I'd stomp and rant, pull my hair, and fume.

My father would point to the house, and off I would trudge.

I remember, however, when it all stopped. My father and I were tossing a ball together, just the two of us, like a scene out of the greatest sports movie ever, *Field of Dreams*. No one was there to see my embarrassment. My father didn't rail against me but rather asked me a simple question: "Do you know why you throw those fits when you make a bad play?"

I thought I knew. I thought I threw those fits because I was angry. But I also knew enough of my father to know he would not ask me a question with a simple answer. And that he would soon enough give me the answer.

"You throw those fits, son, because you are trying to communicate to everyone watching that you are shocked at what has happened. You want them to believe that it is odd, or unusual, for you to drop a pop fly or to boot a ground ball. What you are trying to do is gain a reputation that you have not earned. You want others to think that you are better than you really are."

I was only seven, but I knew wisdom when I heard it.

My father had penetrated my black little heart and shined light on it. His goal, however, was not simply to humiliate me but rather to teach me. He went on.

"Son, I've watched you do the same thing on the golf course. You think you ought to be Arnold Palmer. But you are not Arnold Palmer. Your first name may be Robert, but you are not Roberto Clemente. You are a seven-year-old boy who is just now learning the rudiments of different sports. It takes time to master the skills and to earn a reputation for excellence at them. For now, you need to relax and enjoy the learning. I will be happy to teach you."

That same summer my father worked with me not only on catching and throwing but also on running. The winter prior I had broken a leg skiing, a spiral fracture, that kept me on crutches for three months. When the cast finally came off, I had, in essence, forgotten how to run. My father took me out to the ball field, assessed me as I sprinted from home to first, and offered up his tips. I had been running flat-footed, and he taught me how to run on the balls of my feet.

I still didn't like committing errors out on the field or striking out at bat. But I knew one thing for certain: I didn't want to cheat my way into having a reputation as a good ballplayer. I would live with the reputation I had earned. And after a while, I even earned a reputation as one who was able to keep a cool head in the heat of competition.

It wouldn't be the last time, however, that I would seek shortcuts in acquiring reputation. Nor would it be the last time my father would expose my sin. Yet he always did so tenderly, so that the smoldering wick was not extinguished. He wanted me to learn to be the kind of man he was, and in being both tender toward me and engaged with me, he taught me what kind of father I aspired to be.

My father was truly a Renaissance man. He knew how to touch the consciences of thousands who would read his writing or hear his preaching. But he also knew how to gently goad the conscience of a too-proud little boy. He could plumb the depths of the most challenging theological pickles and grasp the budding mindset of a seven-year-old.

Not only did he teach me theology over the years, but he also pastored me, shepherded me. My wanderings are my fault, not his. My coming home? That's because he always made me feel welcome. I, along with my sister and my mother, were passions of his that never ebbed and flowed. We were never relegated to a garage sale, like the expensive gear in which he would eventually lose interest. Instead, he invested himself in the only things on this earth that will last forever—men's souls.

5

Patriarchal Principle #1

When my family moved from the suburbs of Cincinnati, where my father had served on the staff of College Hill Presbyterian Church, to the Ligonier Valley in rural southwestern Pennsylvania, I—although only six years old—went through some significant culture shock. My parents had both grown up in middle-class homes in Pleasant Hills, a suburb of Pittsburgh. And up till this point, I had lived in the suburbs. I, in short, was the son of suburbanites—and a suburbanite myself. But what awaited me in southwestern Pennsylvania was anything but suburban.

Our new home was along an unpaved stretch of dirt and rocks called Old Distillery Road. It had been named, I presume, during the Prohibition era, when there was probably more moonshine in the hills than sunshine. Forty years after the end of Prohibition, locals still squeezed corn out there. I remember that, as we drove to our new house for the first time, I was less shocked by the unpaved road and more shocked by the lack of sidewalks. Where was I supposed to ride my bike?

My new school, Cook Township Elementary, wasn't a one-room schoolhouse—but it wasn't much more than that. I had classmates there who lived not in a home but in the foundation of a home. Others had no running water, and still others had no electricity. I found myself as a middleclass suburban kid living in the midst of rural poverty. I made friends and adjusted as well as could be expected.

Three years later, however, I went through another culture shock. Concerned about the quality of education I was receiving, my parents took me out of Cook Township Elementary and enrolled me, on a scholarship, at the Valley School of Ligonier. This school was housed in a former mansion that had belonged to part of the Mellon family.

According to the Guinness Book of World Records, the Mellons at that time were the richest family in the world. One of the Mellons was my classmate, and a few others were either ahead of me or behind my grade at the school. I vividly remember seeing a black car, containing the bodyguards of the Mellon kids, follow our bus to school every day.

Having grown up middle class, then having spent a few years in school with people who were less blessed, I experienced a culture shock yet again, being surrounded now by not just money, but by old money. There, at the Valley School of Ligonier, we played soccer in the fall instead of football, lacrosse in the spring instead of baseball. We wore blazers and ties every day.

And we learned Latin.

My father had had a lifelong love affair with Latin. His affections, however, were not returned. This was one of the few realms where his confidence exceeded his abilities—and sometimes, it showed.

At one point he was invited to be the commencement speaker for a small Christian college. There he was honored with his first— although not his last—honorary doctorate. He had determined in advance to address the graduates, the faculty, family, and friends on the serious neglect of study on the work and ministry of the Holy Spirit.

It was a blessed providence that, as he stood to give his address, he noticed the school's motto fit right in with the topic on which he had planned to speak. He read that motto to the assembled—"*Pro Christo et Patria*"—and began with praise. He thought it a marvelous thing, indeed, that the school was built on a commitment to Christ. And, of course, he—having been given to complaining of the church's lack of interest in the character of God the Father—praised them for remembering the Father in their commitment and in their motto.

But where, he wondered out loud, was their commitment to the Holy Spirit? How had the Spirit of the living God—fully God, of the same essence as the Father and the Son—been left off? It was, I am told, quite a passionate address, one not easily forgotten by those in attendance.

When the ceremony ended, the school's president, having conferred on my father that doctorate of letters, had the unenviable task of speaking to him about his address and clarifying a key point. He explained, in gracious terms, that he very much appreciated the call to pay more attention to the Holy Spirit. The thesis was spot-on and much needed. But, he sheepishly explained, the motto of the school, *Pro Christo et Patria*, did not mean, "For Christ and the Father," as my father had mistakenly supposed. It meant, instead, "For Christ and country."

My father's confusion of the Latin word for father (*pater*) and the Latin word for country (*patria*) is understandable enough. A patriot, after all, is one committed to the well-being of his fatherland. The two terms share a common root, and one could even say a common etymology. But they are not at all the same.

This experience, however, did not keep my father from using, and at times misusing, Latin. He delighted in quizzing me on my vocabulary, my declensions, my verb forms. I well remember, however, the first time he dropped a lesser-known Latin derivative (that is, an English word derived from a Latin term) in my lap.

My father, for all his education, was not a stiff and uptight man. Though his intellect may have intimidated some, his demeanor was almost always friendly and welcoming. So I was somewhat surprised when he said to me, very seriously, "Son, I want to give you something, and I want you to hold on to it. Commit it to memory, and live by it. I hereby give you what I will call 'Patriarchal Principle #1...'"

I was two years into my study of Latin, but already this English phrase had me spinning. What, I wondered, was a patriarchal? And if I didn't know already, how important could this soon-to-be-revealed principle actually be?

"This is it," he said, "Patriarchal Principle #1: You don't have to live in a garbage can to know it stinks."

Really? That's it?

I was not, I confess, bowled over. I had no immediate plans for moving into a garbage can. I had never lived in one, neither out of necessity nor out of curiosity as to whether or not it stank. It seemed like a rather unlikely temptation to warn me against, akin to putting a "Beware of tidal waves" sign in the middle of Kansas.

As was so often the case, however, there was a method to my father's madness. I was twelve years old. My voice had already raced through the cracking and croaking stage and had settled into a deep bass tone. Teenage girls I didn't even know would call my phone just to hear me say "hello," giggle, then hang up. Whiskers already protruded from my acne-covered chin. In short, I was already in the hostile wilderness of puberty. I had already taken to experimenting with forbidden pleasures. And my father wanted to dispel the foolish notion that experience is the only true teacher.

Patriarchal Principle #1

My dad never did pronounce to me a Patriarchal Principle #2, but Patriarchal Principle #1, much like Solomon's proverbs, was designed to pass on wisdom, to spare me from having to enroll in the School of Hard Knocks. As a great steward of the gifts God had given Him, he wanted to share his wealth of wisdom with me—wisdom he had learned the hard way through the folly of his own youth.

My father similarly taught me the importance of not only being a steward of what I had been given but of being a steward of my choices. He warned me against being prodigal, against wasting my choices in pursuit of mere experiences. He wanted me to draw interest from the investment of *his* lessons learned. He wanted me to learn to trust the wisdom of my father, even as he was learning to trust the heavenly wisdom of his heavenly Father.

That I haven't always been a good steward is no judgment against my father, who sought to teach me otherwise. Solomon too, whom the Bible has called the wisest man in the world—he who penned so much of the Book of Wisdom—not only had fools for sons but, before all was said and done, had fallen deep into folly himself.

We all need to learn lessons from those who failed to learn their lessons. We don't have to squander what we have been given, nor fight the pigs of this world for scraps, to know that our heavenly Father has so much more for us.

When our heavenly Father warns us, "That stinks; don't go there," a wise will son say, "Yes, sir."

And this is precisely why the one true Wise Son, when facing the raging fires of Gehenna, the wrath of the Father, could wisely say, "Nevertheless, not My will, but Thine be done."

* * *

My father liked to take me to the movies. Usually we went to see the latest blockbuster, but occasionally he would take me to see something a touch more intellectually stimulating. I remember sitting with him in an art house theater to watch Glenn Ford in the seminal teen rebellion movie, *Blackboard Jungle*. Bill Haley's song "Rock Around the Clock" played during the opening credits, connecting the nascent rock-and-roll music with an image of rebellion.

We had a heart-to-heart after we watched this film. My dad explained that, although he had been quite an accomplished athlete in high school, his father's death when he was only seventeen had had a deep impact on him—and not for the better. His anger over his loss had led him to become less of a jock and more of a hoodlum. He had not donned a black leather jacket or ridden a motorcycle, but he had carried a switchblade to school.

His teachers had worried about him, and one found the perfect occasion to get through to him. One day in class, my father picked a fight with one of his classmates. The chip on my father's shoulder clattered to the ground, and my father turned and popped his classmate square in the nose. The fight was over—but not so the consequences.

Blood began to pour, as one might expect. The problem, though, was that the blood was not going to stop. My father had picked a fight with a hemophiliac. The bloodied boy survived the ordeal, but not before being rushed to the hospital.

The teacher of that class was straight out of central casting: Gray hair in a bun, pearl necklace, soft and gentle demeanor. Imagine Helen Hayes with a ruler in hand and a smile on her face. She didn't say a word to my father, save that he was not permitted to leave the classroom until the bloody mess was cleaned up. She went to fetch a bucket, water, soap, and a scrub brush.

Patriarchal Principle #1

When she returned, however, she didn't hand the tools to my father. Instead she got down on her hands and knees, right in front of him, and began to scrub away the blood. The blood he had spilled.

My father heard no ranting, no threatening. But he deeply felt shame at seeing the fruit of his own behavior.

Soon my father's tears joined the water in the bucket, and he pled with her to stop and let him clean up his mess. She gave no answer but just continued with her chore, until the mess was gone.

It was a lesson I know he never forgot, because I heard the pathos in his own voice as he recounted the story to me some thirty years later. And now, as a father myself, I can see the connection between that story and Patriarchal Principle #1. What he learned from his folly was that there were consequences outside his control. Choices made with no forethought too easily result in consequences with no recourse. His loss of temper risked the very life of his classmate.

The quiet suffering of his elderly teacher, however, brings forth fruit to this day. My father learned from watching her. And his son learned from watching her. And now *you* are learning from watching her.

6

Looking for Wisdom in All the Wrong Places

Although we are in union with the divine through the God-Man, Jesus of Nazareth, if we trust in Him alone, there remains a significant difference between Him and us. Although He is our elder brother (Hebrews 2:11), we are still creatures. We are in a battle with sin and with our flesh. Because He has given us new life, however, His Spirit indwells us, and we aspire every day to become more like Him. When we die, John promises that we will be like Him, for we shall see Him as He is (1 John 3:1–3). For now, however, we are called to work at it, to labor to reflect Him.

This is why, I suspect, the shelves of your local Christian bookstore are filled with books providing lessons on how to be more like Him. Two decades or so ago, another fad swarmed over American Christianity, as we all donned bracelets, hats, and T-shirts asking the same question: "WWJD?" or "What Would Jesus Do?"

It's a great question—in its place. There are many things Jesus did, does, and will do, however, that we not only *can't* do but that have no business trying to do. What Jesus did was atone for our sins.

What Jesus does is wash His bride of every blot and blemish. What Jesus will do is bring all things under subjection.

There is, however, one bit of wisdom—built on the notion that we ought to be imitators of Christ—which I have found helpful. When we read of Jesus' public ministry in the Gospels, we are drawn to His stupendous miracles. We are less attracted to the wisdom He spoke into people's lives. And, unfortunately, we practically miss where that all came from.

How often are we told in the Gospels that Jesus went off *alone* to pray?

The "secret"—which really isn't a secret—to the "success" of Jesus' ministry wasn't in His management style, or in His teaching style, or in His preaching style. It was in His spending hours in prayer with His heavenly Father. It's not flashy. It's not complicated. And it is unlikely to ever be the premise of a Christian bestseller. Instead, it is ordinary, common—and yet ever so potent.

I want to be a man like Jesus. And that means I must be a man given to much prayer.

Although Jesus is the greatest man I could ever imitate, He is not the only man I've ever wanted to imitate. Just as Paul encouraged the church at Corinth to imitate *him* as *he* sought to imitate Christ, so too there are men I've admired whom I've wanted to imitate.

In grade school that came out in peculiar ways. I remember studying the various "rituals" of major leaguers when they stepped up to the plate. Joe Morgan would pump his elbow while awaiting the pitch. Richie Hebner would pull and tug at the back collar of his uniform. Willie Stargell would intimidate opposing pitchers by spinning his bat like a windmill.

My favorite player, however, was the "Smiling Panamanian," Manny Sanguillen. Manny was one of the best-hitting catchers of his day. Not only did he not let his own team's errant pitches get past him, but he also didn't let the opposing pitcher's pitches get past him, swinging at just about anything. With each at bat, he stepped into the batter's box, dug both feet in, then raised—one at a time—his spikes and tapped the dirt out with his bat. I mimicked him with every at bat, despite the fact that the dirt didn't get stuck in my sneakers as it did his spikes.

As I grew older and as my father's gifts became more apparent to me, I sought to emulate him as well. While he was a man of prayer who regularly had all-night prayer vigils with student groups when he taught in college, he was also a man of learning, and that is what I, even in junior high school, sought to emulate.

I remember going into his study and slowly spinning in circles. I'm sure there were walls around his office, but you couldn't see them. Each wall was concealed, floor to ceiling, by bookshelves. I would run my eyes over the titles, looking for just the right book. My goal was to acquire wisdom.

The Bible, of course, tells us that the fear of the Lord is the beginning of wisdom. I, however, wasn't looking in the Bible. I thought wisdom came from libraries, like the one in my father's study. I remember my eye being drawn to a couple of slim volumes written by a famous man whose name I had heard. That seemed like the perfect choice for a twelve-year-old. Slim meant easy-to-read. And the fame of the author meant they would bestow wisdom upon me.

I took the books to my bedroom and began to pore over them. When my bedtime came, I curled under the covers and continued to read with a flashlight. My choices were *The Interpretation of Dreams* and *Civilization and Its Discontents*, both by a certain Austrian gentleman named Sigmund Freud.

I doubt there have been many twelve-year-olds sneaking a read of Freud. I also suspect I gleaned roughly the same amount of wisdom as twelve-year-olds who *weren't* reading Freud. To this day, all I remember of what I learned is that I learned and remembered nothing.

Meanwhile, my grades at the elite private school I was attending were not what they could have been. Sure, I did fine, I was never in trouble—but neither did I excel. I had had enough standardized tests to demonstrate that my mediocre grades should have been better. And this led to not one, but many, talks with my father.

Here, though, I fear his grace got the best of him. He would say to me, "Son, your teachers are telling us that your grades do not match your abilities. They all seem to believe that you just aren't putting forth the effort."

Now I was smart enough to know this conversation wasn't going well. I was headed for trouble. But before it ever got there, he rescued me.

"They believe, and I believe," he went on, "that it's because you aren't being sufficiently challenged. The work is too easy to hold your interest."

Whew!

I liked where this was going. It sounded as if he were saying, at one and the same time, that I was a lazy slug who should be ashamed of himself, and that I couldn't help it, that it was the fault of my teachers.

With this line of reasoning, I not only had my previous failures covered but also had a ready-made excuse for future failures: "Sorry about my grades, Dad. I guess my teachers just didn't challenge me enough."

Looking for Wisdom in All the Wrong Places

That didn't work too many times, though, and in part it was Sigmund Freud's fault. It seems that one morning, while getting my sheets ready to be washed, my mother came across not a "gentlemen's magazine," but one of those books by Freud, along with the flashlight I had used to read it. That night at the supper table, my father brought up the discovery.

"Son, your mother found a copy of . . . *Civilization and Its Discontents* . . . in your bed. Now, I'm not saying you shouldn't be reading such a book, but I can't help wondering how it is you find time to read Freud when you're clearly not investing enough time in your actual studies—you know, the reading that has been assigned to you."

I had learned by this time that when you're busted, you're busted. No more lies like the one about the stewed tomatoes. Telling the truth, however, didn't keep me from trying to shine the best possible light on it.

"Dad," I explained, "I understand what you are saying. The thing is, though, not only is the reading for my school assignments less than challenging, but it also doesn't bear much fruit. It's just names and dates, places and factoids. What I'm looking for isn't more information about stuff I frankly don't care about. What I want is wisdom. That's the stuff, Dad: Wisdom. That's why I'm staying up past my bedtime reading Freud, while skating by in my classes."

At that point my father could have praised me for my pursuit of wisdom while scolding me for seeking it in all the wrong places. He could have taken the opportunity to contrast for me true wisdom and what the Bible calls the wisdom of this world. He could have tapped into his own worldview wisdom to expose the folly of Freud.

But that was not what he chose to do. At least not at that moment anyway.

He did, in the end, encourage me for desiring to obtain wisdom. His objection to my method, however, was less about what I had been reading and more about the contrast I had drawn.

"If you want wisdom," he said, "you first must get knowledge. You can have knowledge without wisdom, but it does not follow that you can therefore have wisdom without knowledge. Knowledge is the raw material from which wisdom is built."

Once again, with gentleness, he redirected my steps.

I'd like to say that, from that moment forward, I applied myself to the acquisition of knowledge, and that my grades began to reflect my ability.

But unfortunately that didn't happen.

What did happen was that I stopped looking down my nose at the acquisition of knowledge as somehow beneath me. Better still, I began to look for the connection between knowledge and wisdom. I began, for instance, to understand that learning the history of the Reformation really did help me better grasp Reformed theology, which in turn gave me a deeper appreciation for and understanding of the Bible's central themes. I came to see that biblical history was different from the history I had studied in school, that it was redemptive history: the story of how we are made whole, the story of how Jesus, the Second Adam, is bringing all things under subjection for His honor and glory.

Eventually my dad also dropped some knowledge on me. He gave me a layman's introduction to basic Freudian thought, brilliantly distilling the essence of such concepts as the id, the ego, and the super-ego in a manner that was not only fascinating to hear but also an impressive display of unrehearsed rhetoric. The id, according to Freud was the seat of our most basic desires. The ego was that by which we sought to maintain control of our id. The super-ego was the internalizing of cultural expectations.

Yet, despite my father's best efforts to convey these concepts to me, I did not—and still, to this day, do not—completely understand Freud's human psyche. I did, however, understand it enough to know just what my father meant when he warned me—whenever I would head out the door and away from his supervision—"Keep a lid on the id."

Despite my father's best admonitions, I continued to haunt his study in search of the best books. I soon learned, however, that the ones I benefitted from most were not the ones he had read but the ones he had written. And there's a reason for that. People say that my father's greatest strength as a teacher was his ability to make the complex simple enough for non-experts to understand and to do so without oversimplifying or distorting. That certainly was one of his great strengths.

Greater still, however, were the short lines he drew—for his readers or for his listeners—connecting knowledge and wisdom. He was not a man who would, or even could, separate what he knew academically from how he lived personally.

God, for my father, was not simply an object of study to be understood in intellectual terms. He was the one object of absolute devotion to be pursued. The end goal is never a pointy head filled with knowledge, nor an untethered heart floating about the clouds. Instead the goal is a mind informed, a heart enflamed, both of which lead to hands at work—hands that reflect the tender and scarred hands of our living Savior.

Knowledge is the handmaiden. Wisdom is the queen. And both come together in the Word read, and the Word enfleshed, in Wisdom, the King of heaven and earth.

7

Beyond Freedom and Dignity

It was through Piggy's glasses by which I first saw. There I was, sitting in English class in the eighth grade. Rusty McMullen was the fresh new headmaster of the Valley School, and he was leading us through William Golding's *Lord of the Flies*, a book whose author, a few years later, was awarded the Nobel Prize in Literature. (By the way, if you haven't read *Lord of the Flies*, you should. But I digress.) The book is the account of a group of English schoolboys who find themselves trapped on a deserted island. Where it goes from there is, well, let's just say a descent into chaos—not for the fainthearted, I assure you.

Mr. McMullen (or, "Rusty," as we impertinently called him behind his back) explained to us that when Piggy, a rather appropriately named character in the story, had his glasses broken, it symbolized the loss of civilization, the descent into anarchy. And for me, it became the symbol of my own ascent into a love of reading fiction, of interpreting symbols, of ferreting out worldviews. Four years later I would study English in college, and nine years later pursue a master's degree in English.

Golding was confronting in his work the naive notions of Romantics. And by "Romantics," I am not referring to individuals who like sunset walks on the beach or bouquets teeming with roses, but rather individuals who subscribe to a particular ideology about the nature of man.

Romanticism, birthed out of the folly of eighteenth-century philosopher Jean-Jacques Rousseau, held that man, by nature, is essentially good. The bad that we see, Romantics would argue, isn't the fruit of what we are so much as *where* we are. In other words, it is civilization that is corrupt, and it is civilization that corrupts pure individuals.

Golding confronted this Romantic notion head-on as he took a passel of "innocent" schoolboys and set them free from the shackles of civilization. As you might imagine, Golding's perspective resonated with me, a firm believer in the total depravity of man.

It was at this point that I set aside the ponderous, and often preposterous, musings of Sigmund Freud and his ilk. Instead I turned my attention toward reading novels. It was not, however, a swift transition. Halfway between these genres, I came across a former bestseller that presented psychological theorizing within a fictional format: B. F. Skinner's *Walden Two*.

Skinner was a popular psychologist who, like Carl Sagan and Neil deGrasse Tyson after him, appealed to a wide audience, a lay audience, with his theories. *Walden Two* was a fictionalized account of some skeptics who were coaxed to come and visit a commune set up to follow Skinner's theories.

Some two decades after giving this fictionalized account of his thought, Skinner published a nonfiction work that described and defended his version of behaviorism, a view that says we are what we are because we have been conditioned to be that way by our environment. Its provocative title was *Beyond Freedom and Dignity*.

My father had learned the importance of not leaving my reading unscrutinized. I noted earlier that, while I had not been homeschooled, my father always showed an active and avid interest in my education. We would be at the dinner table, and, after he had given my mother a stroke-by-stroke rundown of his afternoon on the golf course, he would ask me about my classes. He was delighted when we read *Lord of the Flies* for class, but he was not always delighted with the books I tracked down on my own.

The appeal of Rousseau, and the complementary appeal of Skinner, is easy enough to grasp. If I am inherently good but act badly, and if it is the fault of society that I'm acting badly, then any guilt I feel is unnecessary and misguided. If, as Skinner argued, I am neither more nor less than the combined influences of the environment around me, then again, I have no need to worry about guilt. My sins are not my fault but rather the fault of my environment. Blame is banished, responsibility is banished—and with them, dignity is banished.

There is, however, an added element of the sinister that Skinner adds to the equation. With Rousseau, the path to paradise lies in inactivity, in keeping civilization at bay, rather than in building it. With Skinner, however, there is a fight to control the environment of others so that others can be controlled. C. S. Lewis grasped this, noting in his potent and prophetic book *The Abolition of Man*, "What we call Man's power over Nature turns out to be a power exercised by some men over other men with Nature as its instrument."[4]

In both *Walden Two* and *Beyond Freedom and Dignity*, Skinner subtly and ironically seeks to appeal to the ego, to the pride of the reader. As he describes our utter helplessness in the face of our environments, he wants us to think as well of the utter helplessness others would have if we were to control their environments. It is almost as if he wants us to imagine the Soviet Union as a kind of utopia, not because everyone is well taken care of, but because we are at the top of a tyrannical pyramid.

Skinner's program faces not just a critical moral dilemma but a logical one as well. If it is true that we are all under the sway and control of our environments, then the only reason we believe we are under the sway and control of our environments is because our environments have told us so. That is, if humans really have no control over their choices, then we have no control over whether or not we believe we have control over our choices. To put it still another way, if Skinner can control the rest of us by manipulating our environments, then he too must be under the control of his environment. Got that? Okay, one more time. Let's try it this way: If we are all mere puppets, then none of us can climb our strings in order to control the other puppets.

Eventually, when I grew a bit older, my father explained all that to me, how Skinner's worldview was utterly self-defeating. But that evening he took a more direct approach with me. He determined not to answer the fool Skinner according to his folly. Instead he asked me a simple but powerful question.

"Do you know, son," he asked pensively, "what lies beyond freedom and dignity?"

"No, sir."

"Slavery and indignity."

He swiftly and unambiguously ripped the mask off Skinner's title and exposed his nefarious agenda. *Beyond*, after all, is a word we tend to associate with progress, with improvement. When we learn new things, we move beyond the elementary principles. When we board our spaceships, we explore the great beyond. Skinner had hitched his wagon to the Enlightenment Project—human evolution to ever bigger and better things.

To get there, according to Skinner, we have to cast off not just our religious prejudices, which only serve to hold us back, but even our unscientific notions of freedom and human dignity. We are, according to Skinner, what my father would often describe as "grown-up germs." We began as a cosmic accident; we end up as dust. The naive and happy humanist notion that, between these two poles of utter insignificance, we are imbued with such things as rights, value, and dignity, is laughable. If, my father used to say, we are but grown-up germs, who cares whether the white germs or the black germs have to sit in the back of the bus?

The heady promise of Enlightenment optimism is, in the end, nothing more than the hollow promise of the serpent in the Garden of Eden. Toss aside freedom and dignity, and you will find nothing better, just slavery and indignity. My father was warning me never to trade my birthright for any mess of pottage, no matter how pleasing to the eye it might look.

* * *

My father's rhetorical skills, combined with his good intentions, gave him the capacity to embrace the call of our Lord that we be "as wise as serpents and harmless as doves" (Matthew 10:16). He knew how words could be used to entice and beguile, but when they're used that way, they conceal the hard truth that the rose is made of plastic while the thorn is all too real. His desire was always to use language to unveil, rather than to veil, the truth. He understood that plain speaking is always a powerful antidote to flowery rhetoric.

Better still, he was reminding me of an important truth, a truth grasped by our Founding Fathers. Our liberties are not things that wax and wane depending on the latest political winds. It is because we are made in God's image, even those who deny that we are made in God's image, that we have dignity. This is why our Founding Fathers affirmed that our rights are not mediated to us via our elected leaders but are rather inalienable rights endowed to us by our Creator. In other words, since no man has bestowed these inalienable rights on us, no man can take them away.

This reminds me of something else my father said, years later, something I never forgot. It was his habit, from time to time, and a habit I have adopted with fervor, to use a particular rhetorical tool wherein he would say something totally shocking, something orthodoxy would condemn as outright heresy. Then, having his audience members at the edges of their seats, he would carefully explain why what he had just spoken was both true and orthodox. More often than not, he would even take me in.

I remember him speaking at a conference and insisting, with utmost certainty, that we are in fact justified by works. He repeated his contention not once, not twice, but multiple times—insisting that, at the very foundation, our salvation is based on works. In the moment I honestly thought he was having a most inopportune brain hiccup. Surely he was just forgetting the all-important "not"— justified *not* by works but by faith.

Not wanting to leave folks, myself included, in a state of bewilderment and disbelief, he went on to explain that God deems us righteous not only because of the atoning work of Christ on the cross but also because of the righteous life that Christ lived in our place. That is to say, the work of Christ is indeed appropriated by faith alone and not by works—and, yet, it is the *work* of Christ that justifies.

On a different occasion, in his systematics class, he helped us all better understand the dignity of man. He began by insisting that our value is not intrinsic, that there is no such thing as the inherent sacredness of human life. There is nothing innate in us that is of any value. That day, I, along with the rest of the class, was silently screaming, "But what about the *imago Dei*? What about the glorious truth that we are made in the image of God?" Fortunately he didn't torture us too long before he turned it all around.

"You may be thinking, 'But what about the *imago Dei*?'" he said. "That is indeed where human dignity resides, and it is absolutely true that every human being bears that image. What you have to grasp however, is that the *imago* is extrinsic to us. It is from outside of us. It is imprinted on us by God. It is universal, but it is not innate. It is the grace of God."

My father was a man who did not merely affirm the universal dignity of man as a cold, brute fact. He was a man who expressed great delight in communing with other fellow image-bearers, treating every person with unparalleled dignity. He was the kind of man who treated others—whether employees of his ministry, servers at his favorite restaurant, or strangers on a train—as what they truly were: human beings made in the image of God. Men, women, and children with value, with aspirations. He understood, again, the wisdom of C. S. Lewis, who said of man in his *The Weight of Glory*:

> It is a serious thing to live in a society of possible gods and goddesses, to remember that the dullest most uninteresting person you can talk to may one day be a creature which, if you saw it now, you would be strongly tempted to worship, or else a horror and a

corruption such as you now meet, if at all, only in a nightmare. All day long we are, in some degree helping each other to one or the other of these destinations. It is in the light of these overwhelming possibilities, it is with the awe and the circumspection proper to them, that we should conduct all of our dealings with one another, all friendships, all loves, all play, all politics. There are no ordinary people. You have never talked to a mere mortal. Nations, cultures, arts, civilizations—these are mortal, and their life is to ours as the life of a gnat. But it is immortals whom we joke with, work with, marry, snub, and exploit—immortal horrors or everlasting splendors.[5]

8

My Hometown

Given my idyllic upbringing, I'm not quite sure where or how cynicism first took root in me. I do know, however, that it blossomed over the course of my high school days, beginning when I was fourteen.

That year was a good year for me, a year in the local public school after attending Valley School and before heading several states away to attend another highbrow private academy. During that school year, I began to understand my parents' concern about the academic quality of the local government education; I literally never took a book home to do a homework assignment that year, yet I was able to remain near the top of my class.

My time and energy were devoted instead to sports and to my social life. I played football in the fall, starting both ways, as fullback and as linebacker. In the winter I played basketball, starting not at all. In the spring it was soccer, and, for the first time, I was able to play my natural position—goalie.

The first sign of my budding cynicism probably showed up at the dinner table. As always, my father took time to inquire about my studies, about each day at school. Our routine later became part of one of his talks on the sovereignty of God in creation. He explored therein the nature of creation *ex nihilo*, creation out of nothing, by examining just what nothing is—or, rather, isn't.

He cited the Puritan giant Jonathan Edwards, who said that nothing is what sleeping rocks dream of. Nothing, my father opined, despite being too small to be measured, is a difficult concept to get our heads around. Then, he explained, he finally learned just what nothing is, from me, at the dinner table. He would ask what I had done at school that day, and I'd reply, "Nothin'."

"Nothing," he would tell the gathered crowd, "is what my son did in school each day in the ninth grade."

I wasn't hostile toward my dad in my response. I wasn't even sullen yet (although that would come later). I was just indifferent. My interests were my own, and they didn't include the material being covered in my ninth-grade classrooms. My cynicism likely began around my understanding of education. I was not mad that success came easily at my new school or that I was not being challenged adequately. I was mad that I was going to have to leave.

The picture I got from my parents was that you have to attend a competitive high school, so you can get into a competitive college, so you can get into a competitive graduate school, so you can get a high-paying job, so you can live in a neighborhood that has competitive high schools, so that, a generation later, your children can start running on the same hamster wheel.

Whether it was the overall futility of the plan, or the simple fact that I would soon have to leave my home and my family, I wasn't having it.

I had come to embrace my rural life. I had developed an aesthetic sensibility that could take in the beauty of the forest, the sublimity of the mountains, and breathe easy. The suburbs, conversely, were organized living for organization men. And I wanted nothing to do with that.

Until my father said to me, "Son, let's take a walk."

And so naturally, he and I took a walk.

As I have already mentioned, both my parents grew up in Pleasant Hills, a bedroom community just outside Pittsburgh. There was nothing peculiar about this suburb. "Suburb" is about all you need to know to get the picture.

Neither of my father's parents were alive by the time I was two days old. My mom's parents, however, lived in the very same home she had grown up in. Since they were little more than an hour from our home, we visited them often.

Although a busy road ran less than twenty yards from their front door, their neighborhood had a few charms. Every weekday morning and afternoon, you could watch hordes of schoolchildren—not waiting for a bus, but walking to school and back. (I learned, contrary to what my parents had told me, that it actually wasn't "uphill both ways.") On Sundays, the local church, just four blocks away—the church where my parents had grown up—rang its steeple bells to call the community to worship. Men in suits and ties, women in hats and white gloves, followed the same sidewalks their children took to attend school.

It was still, however, suburbia. And I turned my nose up at it. It seemed too sterile, too impersonal, too inorganic.

I did not, however, have any intention of missing this walk with my father. I knew I was in no danger of getting in trouble, that he had just asked because he wanted my company. We stepped out the door, and my father began to tell me about the family who had once lived directly across the street. He hadn't, however, gotten two sentences out before discovering that they still lived there.

"Sonny?" a voice queried from the screened-in porch.

When my father was growing up in his home, there had been his father, Robert; an uncle, also Robert; and an older sister, Roberta. Before he became known as R. C., my father had been known as Sonny.

We crossed the busy road and visited. My father and his friends recounted old stories, sharing laughs. Hardships were shared as well. These were people whose lives had intersected my parents' lives for forty years. After some iced tea, we headed out to continue our journey.

Not much, however, changed along the way. My father pointed out various homes of various families, only to discover that the same families were still there. We stopped in multiple homes and had multiple conversations. Over the course of four hours, we probably hadn't covered more than six blocks. But we had stopped to interact with more than half-a-dozen old friends, each of them friendly, warm, and best of all, familiar to my father.

As we progressed, I began to get a picture of my parents as children, and then as teenagers, above and beyond the stories my father had told me about his youthful exploits at sports and that, up until this point, had populated my understanding of his youth. My parents had had a life before me, a life with real people in it, people who knew them and cared about them. They also had had a life before he was *the* R. C. Sproul. When he was just Sonny.

Our journey ended around the corner at the local Buick dealership. And there, we met Johnny.

Johnny had been my father's best friend growing up. They had done everything together. They had even gone off to college together. One day, during their first semester there, they planned a trip across the state line into Ohio where, not coincidentally, eighteen-year-olds could purchase alcohol legally. Before leaving, however, they stopped in the student lounge to buy cigarettes from a vending machine. The captain of the football team was there in discussion with several other students, and he invited Johnny and my dad to join them.

There, despite having grown up in that neighborhood church, my father heard the gospel for the first time. He and Johnny were both transfixed, Johnny making a profession of faith that very night. Ohio could wait. My father, however, was not so eager—not because he hadn't been captured by the message, but because he had. That is, he knew that such a decision wasn't a small thing, but everything.

The next morning, like a late-night reveler who awakes wondering what he has done the night before, Johnny dropped his commitment to Christ.

The next night, my father picked up his cross and followed Him.

It should be noted that my father, a few weeks after crying out for the mercy of God in Christ, spoke to his pastor during a weekend away from school. He sat in the pastor's august office, pouring out his heart about his conviction of sin and about the glorious release at the foot of the cross.

The pastor responded, "If you believe in the resurrection of Jesus, you're a damned fool." A stunning response from a pastor regarding what Christians have always affirmed to be the corner-stone of Christian doctrine. After all, following the death of Judas, the apostles thought it necessary to complete their number again by including one who was a witness to Jesus' bodily resurrection (Acts 1:21–22). This truth was the one point Peter emphasized in his seminal sermon on the Day of Pentecost; it was also the central doctrine of the apostle Paul in his famous Mars Hill address, as well as central to his teaching ministry. No, the fool in the office that day was not the one who embraced the bodily resurrection of Jesus from the dead, but the one who denied its historical reality.

And now, for the first time in decades, my father and Johnny were together again at the Buick dealership as we walked through Pleasant Hills. Their love for each other was obvious, but so were the differences of the paths they had taken.

My father was married to my mom, his childhood sweetheart. His ministry was taking off. Johnny, however, was a shadow of what he had been. Divorce had sapped his strength and drained his bank account, and he was left trying to eke out a living selling used cars. There was a deep sorrow in Johnny's eyes, a longing for what might have been. I could almost see the thorns and thistles that had choked the life out of him.

We said our goodbyes, but that was not to be the last I would hear of Johnny.

Not long after that walk, my father began work on what may have been his most shocking book, *Johnny Come Home*, a thinly veiled novel telling the story of two best friends who heard the gospel and took different paths. I looked up Johnny ten years later and found him at the same dealership, still selling cars, still with the same haunted look in his eyes.

My dad and I made our way back to my grandparents' house. I felt like I had just lived through a lifetime of change. I had seen not just suburbia but my parents in a whole new light. They were no longer just my mother and my father; they were people, real humans. And the folks marrying, giving birth, growing old in their planned half-acre lots—they too, I realized, were people. They were not merely props, not just background clutter in the lives of important people. They were important; they were people.

Whether you live on fifty acres of wooded splendor, in a third-floor walk-up, or somewhere in between, you bear the image of God. You think—whether you articulate them or not—heavy thoughts. You ponder deep questions, live with profound fears, and dream great dreams. There are no little people—apart from the people who think, like I did once, that some people are little.

Each and every one of us will one day be either in eternal torment or in eternal bliss.

You may be waiting for some profound comment from my father that cemented the lesson that day, that drove it from my mind to my heart. You may be anticipating a nugget of wisdom, suitably pithy and brief enough to fit on a plaque or in a tweet.

If that's the case, you missed it. For these were the words he spoke that shaped me, molded me, remade me: "Son, let's go for a walk."

My father had no grand plan that afternoon. He wasn't trying to teach me anything in particular, which is how, often, the best lessons in life are learned. Instead he did what every father should do with every son—he welcomed me into his world. He showed me the world that had shaped him.

His world wasn't built around mannequins or Stepford wives. It wasn't precanned and saccharine. It was honest and real. His world was as real as the lesson I was learning, as natural as a son taking a walk with his father. I knew from that day forward that I didn't know what kind of work I would be called to do when I was fully grown, but that I did know I wanted my neighbors to remember me as my father's neighbors remembered him. I wanted to know them, and to be known by them. And I knew that I could have that—if I worked at it—wherever God would place me.

Today, I know this as well. Sonny is home, where he should be, knowing he is known and loved as he never was before. And Johnny, if you're out there, it's time for you to come home too. The fatted calf is waiting. The robe is pure and clean. And the ring bears the signet of the King.

Come home, Johnny. Come home.

9

Dreaded Locks

Reading Freud in my teenage years did little more than introduce me to the grammar, the basic terms, of his thought. Despite my best efforts to enjoy his writings, I became thoroughly convinced that diving more deeply into Freud's works was not in my immediate future.

Somewhere along the line, however, I came across Freud's notion of the Oedipal complex, named after the ancient Greek play *Oedipus Rex*. The play tells the story of a baby prophesied to kill his father and marry his mother. As an infant he is set to sea, to keep the prophecy from coming to pass. Of course, that very act set the stage for the fulfillment of the prophecy. When he is grown, Oedipus unknowingly returns to his homeland, accidentally kills his father, and ends up marrying his mother.

Freud argued that boys see their fathers as competition for the affection of the mother/wife. That, happily, was never a problem either of us had. Instead, we both gave thanks for my mother's love, his wife's love, for us both.

That did not mean, however, that my father and I never competed with each other. Remember how I noted that when it came to sports, all I really had to offer was knowledge of the games and an iron will? That iron will came out in everything—sports, games, cards, you name it. If there were a contest, I didn't merely aspire to compete; I wanted to win. Second place, in my mind, was just a kinder way of saying "the first loser."

I eventually discovered, however, that there are some things worse than losing—like winning.

My father's athletic skills sometimes surprised people who only knew him as an older man. Age, genetics, and perhaps too much cake and ice cream led to my father's developing a bit of a bubble in his midriff. None of that, however, undid his guns. As a boy I would beg my father to make a muscle, and I would delight in its size and recalcitrance. When I grew older, my father would flex his forearms, honed by hours and hours on the golf course, and ask me, "Have you ever known a theologian with forearms like these?"

I delighted in my father's strength, but I also desired to compete with him. That competition often took the form of arm wrestling. Like Rocky Balboa in his first movie, I wasn't dumb enough to think I could beat him. I just wanted to go the distance. The longer I could withstand him, the better I felt about myself. Eventually, however—much like Rocky—I came to believe that I actually could win.

I was fifteen and just beginning to realize that my father was not immune to the ravages of time. I was getting stronger, and he was getting weaker. With each arm-wrestling match, I drew closer and closer. Though I hated to lose, I found myself challenging him more and more frequently. He, knowing what was coming, would try to beg off. (About this same time, we also played a fair amount of one-on-one basketball. He insisted, however, that we only play to three, because he knew his skill advantage would be no match in a longer game against my endurance advantage.)

Dreaded Locks

One day, the long-anticipated moment finally arrived. My mother just so happened to be there to see it, as well as my sister. There my dad and I were, locked in mortal combat, our hands squeezing each other's as, slowly, inch by inch, my dad's arm dropped closer and closer to the kitchen table. Finally, his arm touched. I was ecstatic, overjoyed, stunned. I had won. I had beaten him. I thanked him for the competition, took a shower (for it wasn't an easy thing to beat him, and I was covered in sweat), and went to bed.

Whatever joy I had at beating my father was soon replaced by a sense of melancholy. I lay there in growing agony, crying myself to sleep. These were not tears of joy, but tears of deep sorrow and despondency. There was something tragic about it all—the inevitability of age, the switching of roles. No, my victory didn't make me the head of our house. But my victory did mean that if there was any heavy lifting that needed to be done, the job was now mine.

The real problem was that I actually got what I had wanted: to beat my dad. And now I realized that I hated it. He was my dad; I didn't want to be stronger than him.

While his physical prowess succumbed to the inevitable decay of nature, his mind, by contrast, never lost its potency. Not long after his dethroning as arm-wrestling champ of the household, we had another battle, this one of wits. I learned quickly enough what my father was already keenly aware of: that he was battling against a one-armed man.

It was my first trip home after going off to private school in Wichita. It was spring break. My parents met me at the gate of Pittsburgh International Airport. My father was not as effusive as I was accustomed to. I could tell he had something on his mind. We picked up my bag and walked to the car in silence.

As my father pulled away, his tires chirped as he hit the gas. Now I knew something was wrong—really wrong. That was not like him at all. Finally the silence was broken when he said to my mother, through clenched teeth, "We need to stop on the way home to get him a haircut." When she suggested that that could probably wait, he turned his attention to me.

He launched into a tirade in which he rebuked me for deliberately trying to provoke him. It was a self-conscious decision I had made, he informed me, to spit in his eye by growing my hair long. He demanded to know what he had done that had made me so angry at him that I would slap him in the face by growing out my hair.

I was utterly baffled.

The sad truth is that, over the years, I had committed all manner of sins that I knew would displease my father. I had pursued illicit pleasures, against his express command. But I understood that old saying, "Hypocrisy is the homage that vice pays to virtue." My dishonesty had always been grounded in something completely honest: I wanted my pleasures, to be sure, but I never wanted to bring shame to my father or mother through them. I did things they opposed, but never in an attempt to oppose them.

I lived, like too many others, with one foot in the kingdom and one foot in the world, trying to eat my poison cake and have it too. I was foolish, undisciplined, certainly a lover of my belly—but one thing I was not was a son who would intentionally spit in his father's eye. I loved my father dearly, and I wanted him to be proud of me.

I had the good sense, at the end of his tirade, to not fight fire with fire. A soft answer, the Bible tells us, turns away wrath. That is exactly what I aimed to do when I explained to my father that my hair being long had nothing to do, whatsoever, with seeking to get under his skin. My decision was not rooted in rebellion against him, at least not consciously.

Fighting back the tears I felt starting to overpower me, I choked up, telling him that not only was I not seeking to offend him but that I wanted him to be proud of me. I let him know I was sorry it had so offended him, and I assured him that offending him was the last thing I had hoped to do.

"If you aren't trying to offend me," he responded coolly, "can you tell me what led you to make this choice? Why have you grown your hair long, if not as a sign of rebellion?"

My answer reveals just how spiritually immature my thinking was, justifying my actions under the guise of personal piety. I wanted to be honest with him, even if it was embarrassing to admit, so I shared with him my rationale.

"Dad," I began, "you have to understand what it's like out there. My classmates—they're not like me, not at all. Their interests run to cars, to girls, to arcade games. They are shallow people, living shallow lives."

My cynicism by now was in full bloom, as you can see, and so was my foolish pride.

"They are cookie-cutter kids," I continued, "and I just don't want to look like them. I want to look different from them, so people will know I'm not like them."

What I did not want at the moment was any more discussion on the issue. But the conversation wasn't over. My response had not assuaged my father's disapproval of my long hair, as I had naively hoped it would. With his words tender and gracious, and his purpose didactic, he used the opportunity to point me to the glory and grace of God.

"Son, I can understand how you would feel that way," he said. "I even understand why you would want to communicate to others what you are trying to communicate. What you don't seem to understand, however, is that the message you are seeking to get across is not the message you are sending. When people see a young man with long hair, they jump to the conclusion that such a man is at the very least in rebellion, likely a drug user, and maybe even a drug dealer. You need to think not just about what you are saying but about what others are *hearing*."

In my sophomoric pride, I was persuaded I now had him dead to rights. Yes, all our lives, I had lost every single argument we'd ever had. But just as I had vanquished him in arm wrestling, so now I believed I would drop the hammer on him—kindly and gently of course, but still I believed I would claim my crown as the king of logic.

"Dad, I understand what you are saying," I patiently explained. "People are so quick to judge and to jump to conclusions. But surely you don't expect me to adapt myself to the folly of others. I mean, if someone were fool enough to judge me on the basis of my hair, of all things, should I really even take that into account?"

Case closed. Not even my father could refute that airtight logic. Moreover, I convinced myself, my dad had sided with the shallow people—those hasty, judgmental people—and I had connected with the broadminded, the kind, the gracious. I felt a sense of pity for him, that he had let himself succumb to emotion over reason.

That is, until, he went into his Columbo routine. He scratched his head and looked puzzled.

"Do you mind if I ask you a question?" he began. "Am I mistaken, or is it not the case that, just a few minutes ago, you were telling me that the very reason, the core motivation, as to why you grew your hair, was precisely because you *wanted* people to judge you by your hair?"

With that one simple question, my father had settled it. All I could say in response was, "Anywhere you want to stop for a haircut is fine with me."

I knew I had been beaten. Not just beaten, but embarrassed. He chopped logic with the best of them, and I was only an amateur. My king was in checkmate, and every one of my pieces was sitting on the table beside him. I have, since then, lost plenty of arguments—but never quite so thoroughly.

Just as I had moved from euphoria to mourning over defeating my father in arm wrestling, so now I moved from shame to joy over losing this argument. My father had a steel-trap mind, and it was a beautiful thing to watch it in action, even if that trap was snapping shut on my shoulder-length hair. He was the master, and I was just an apprentice—albeit an apprentice privileged to study at the feet of the master.

In the same way his bulging biceps had comforted me as a boy, making me believe that, if push came to shove, my dad really could beat up the dads of the other kids on my block, so now I was comforted in knowing that the convictions my father had poured into me were bulwarked by his astute mind. Sure, I may not have been smart enough to defend the things I believed, but I knew someone who was smart enough to do so—and someone who was a world-class defender of what we, together, believed.

Shortly after my father's mentor, Dr. John Gerstner, passed into glory, I remember my father telling me how it brought him both sorrow and fear. He would miss the man who had been a spiritual father to him, but he also felt the loss of saying goodbye to his own go-to guy whenever he was stumped by a question, thinking through an argument, or wrestling with a doubt. As he confessed that little-known secret to me, I remember thinking that I too would one day experience that same sense of sorrow and fear. My hero and champion missed his hero and champion—and today, I now know what that feels like.

That day, as I arrived home from Kansas, I was grateful, knowing that my father could not only answer the folly of unbelievers and skeptics but that he could also unearth and answer my own folly. He was my guardrail. And I miss him dearly.

10

My Droogs

My youth, like most people's, was a heady time of new experiences, of spreading my wings. What was perhaps unusual was that, as a teen, I did not rebel against the convictions of my parents but, by God's grace, began to own them more and more fully as my own. That led to the dual blessing not only of being sounder in my thinking but also of being more fully in fellowship with my family.

First I grew in my capacity to understand my father's teachings. I listened to his lectures on audiotapes, read his books and manuscripts, and from time to time traveled with him. Our conversations broadened beyond sports and beyond what I was—or wasn't—doing in school.

It may well be that my father let me more fully into his world through our seeing *Star Wars* together. He, having grown up on Errol Flynn's swashbuckling adventures, saw in the movie a blockbuster action epic. I, newly anointed in the esoteric art of reading symbols in fiction, unpacked those parts of the movie that were a bit more subtle than exploding planets or the detonation of the Death Star.

Much like his logic-chopping over my hair or the intensity he brought to our arm-wrestling matches, my father's growing respect for me did not lead to his retirement from the battlefield but rather to more focus in competition. Seeing my game get better, he upped his game. And just as he had put me in my place over my hair, so too he now snatched the movie critic trophy from me—which left me, not bitter, but grateful and in awe.

By the time I reached my high school years, my parents had developed a pattern of spending several months each year in the solitude of the Arizona desert. There my father was afforded the time to complete a book, free from the daily distractions of running a worldwide ministry. I visited during the Thanksgiving and Christmas breaks. I didn't particularly care for the heat, nor for the decorated potted palm vainly trying to pass as a Christmas tree. But I loved being there with them, sharing life with them.

One year my father took me to the Fiesta Bowl, where I had the privilege of watching my Penn State Nittany Lions embarrass the Ohio State Buckeyes. What could be any better for a dedicated college football fan? And, believe it or not, I had Chinese food for the first time, there in Arizona. My trips to Arizona were always seemingly nonstop visits packed with time together. Most enjoyable were our daily tennis matches and then lounging in the hot tub at the complex where my parents stayed.

It was during one of these annual trips that our family drove through the desert to San Diego for the Congress on the Bible conference where I met Josh McDowell. What stands out amongst all the adventures, however, was an afternoon trip we took to the movies. My father wasn't always the most cautious man in choosing movies. I remember having given thanks just a few years before for the theater's darkness since it hid my blushing face while the four of

My Droogs

us—my mom, my dad, my sister, and I—watched a scene that was, to say the least, not appropriate for younger audiences. Apparently he did not learn much from that experience, because now, several years later, he was taking me to see *A Clockwork Orange*.

As an aside, I am a bit put off by the fact that people refer to this movie as Stanley Kubrick's *A Clockwork Orange*. Three years prior, Kubrick had made it big with *2001: A Space Odyssey*, so having his name attached to *A Clockwork Orange* was simply good marketing. The movie is based on a book by British critic, composer, linguist, and novelist Anthony Burgess. To Kubrick's credit, many people—including myself—would likely never have been introduced to Burgess were it not for Kubrick's movie, but surely this film should be called "Anthony Burgess's *A Clockwork Orange*, directed by Stanley Kubrick."

Burgess set his account in the future, in a world where young thugs are on the loose. The antihero, Alex, is a ruffian given to drug use, murder, rape. Eventually he is captured and imprisoned for his crimes. Through the machinations of several competing interests—all of which demonstrate that even the "responsible" law-abiding people in the story had their own internal wickedness—Alex is put into a program built around aversion therapy.

For starters, he is strapped to a chair, administered drugs that make him violently nauseated, and with his eyes forced open made to watch nonstop films depicting gratuitous violence and sexual assaults—the very crimes he himself had willingly committed. As he undergoes this therapy, Beethoven's Ninth Symphony plays in the background, thus destroying Alex's one redeeming quality: his appreciation for fine music.

The therapy "works" and Alex is "cured." What he has lost, however, is all that gave him life. Replacing his humanity is a dull apathy that results in his becoming a drone and, in the end, a victim.

His former friends have been recruited into the police force where brutality reigns. Worse still, Alex is captured by the husband of one of his victims. The husband, still reeling from the crime Alex had committed against his loved one, traps him in a room and booms the music of Beethoven through massive speakers, torturing Alex with what he once loved.

Kubrick's presentation of those parts of the movie that had initially earned it an X-rating at its original release, ten years before I saw it, was anything but titillating. While we were encouraged, in the end, to feel a kind of sympathy for the protagonist, there was nothing sympathetic about his crimes. I didn't walk out of the theater thinking how cool my father was for letting me see such a gratuitous display of depravity.

Later, over dinner and conversation about the movie, I sat and listened as my father delivered a full-orbed lecture on the origin, premises, and errors that made up behaviorist ideology. I ate up every word. He went on to explain how the movie portrayed the dehumanizing effect of behavioral thinking. It was an important movie that had as its message an important rebuttal of a secular worldview. Alex was reprogrammed and, in being reprogrammed, he lost his humanity. There is a scene near the end of the movie in which Alex is in a hospital bed, talking with the doctor who had performed the procedure of reprogramming him. The doctor cuts up Alex's food as Alex opens his mouth to be fed. He is an infant once more.

I was accustomed to my father's theological precision by this point in my life. I had heard him preach numerous gripping sermons. But there, as we discussed *A Clockwork Orange* over dinner, I thought I was sitting across from Francis Schaeffer or C. S. Lewis: scintillating commentary on serious cinema, complete with sound biblical critique, exposing the inherent flaws in the dominant worldview around us. And I was getting it all over dinner. My father acted like it was no big deal, just a normal day for him. That's because it was a normal day for him, no big deal.

People have asked me from time to time how my father was so gifted at finding compelling illustrations of deep theological truths from everyday experiences to which any person could relate. The answer is that the question itself is upside down. My father didn't take a theological idea in all its abstract nakedness and then search for something real and concrete to explain it. Rather, he always looked at everything in light of his theological convictions. He didn't see the world as a closet full of potential illustrations. Instead he saw all of life as the outworking of a worldview. He didn't, because it was a Kubrick film, put on his critic's hat. It's just the way he was.

While my father's keen insight should have provoked me to greater heights of relationship with him, I must confess that I allowed it to have the opposite effect. To say that I was utterly impressed by my father's insight, by his powers of perception, by his discernment, is to tell only half the story. The truth is that my newfound awareness of the depth of my father's ability to perceive reality led me to shy away from him, for fear that he could see into the darkest corners of my soul. Being around him often felt like going through the dessert buffet with your nutritionist peering over your shoulder as you reach for more.

That is not to say he was given to criticism. Quite the opposite. He was always given to encouragement, and that to a fault. A few years prior to our movie outing, I had had my heart set on becoming a mountain man, like Grizzly Adams. My father had encouraged me, waiting patiently for me to mature enough to realize how impractical a goal that was. In time, I moved on to another dream—I wanted to be a lumberjack. It was the best combination of mountain man and practicality I could imagine. Again, my father encouraged me.

Still not permanently settled on a career choice, I changed my life's goal once again after I obtained my driver's license. This time I was sure I wanted to become a truck driver. Why not? I loved driving, and I loved listening to music, and clearly truck driving would be a wonderful way to get paid to doing what I loved. Again, he encouraged me.

Eventually I realized that whatever notion I came up with, he would encourage me. I'm sure that if I had ever said, "Dad, I think I'd like to be a rodeo clown," he would have cleared the way for me to make it happen. Which, of course, discouraged me. I never knew whether his enthusiasm for what I did, or said, or planned, was genuine, or just a natural outflowing of his general desire to be a Barnabas, a son of encouragement.

I put him in a tough place. I began, little by little, to pull back, lest he see things in me that he would disapprove of. And at the same time, I grew a bit skeptical of the approval he was prone to give me. I don't think I quite got over my immature fear until decades later.

* * *

Several years after we saw *A Clockwork Orange* in the theater, my father and I were having a conversation. I don't remember all the details of the conversation, but I do vividly remember at some juncture trying to make a point, and doing so by way of illustration. The illustration itself was from a moment I was confident neither of us would ever forget, for it had definitely stuck with me.

"Remember when we were in that meeting," I said, "with a dozen or so Ligonier employees? We were trying to solve some problem, and you made a suggestion you thought would help solve the problem. I thought it wasn't such a good idea, and right there—in front of people who reported to me, and people to whom I reported, all of whom ultimately reported to you—I blurted out indignantly, 'Are you out of your mind?' Do you remember when that happened?"

His answer was immediate: "No, I don't remember that."

Now, I don't know whether he honestly didn't remember, or if he was just trying to help me put my shame behind me. Either way, that's the kind of man he was. He did not hold many grudges. He was quick to forgive, and even quicker to forget. But he was also sensitive to the delicate consciences of others.

If I had to choose—did he forget? or did he simply want me to think he had forgotten?—I would choose the former. Several years after that moment, I was talking with my father again, and I was trying to encourage him. I was telling him about what I've just told you, about how I was so utterly blown away by his assessment of Stanley Kubrick's film. His response caught me off guard. He did not thank me for the encouraging words, as I had thought he would.

Instead he looked at me in bewilderment.

"I've never seen *A Clockwork Orange*," he said.

I tried to jog his memory, to describe what he had had to say about it, but he wouldn't budge. He was adamant he had never seen the movie, let alone taken his son to see it with him. Perhaps embarrassment for letting me view such a controversial movie drove it from his memory. More likely, however, it meant so much less to him than it did to me, and so it slipped his mind.

To be sure, it is not something that I held against him. Rather, his inability to recall seeing the movie is just a small bit of evidence that what I experienced as extraordinary—his incredible commentary on the film—was utterly ordinary for him. He had no reason to remember such a mundane course of events, because every day was like that for him.

And this is where so much of the real blessing was in being his son. Anyone could listen to the sermons, read the books, or attend the conferences. But I got the table talk.

11

Whatcha Got?

Before James Dean's star-turning roll as a troubled, angst-riddled teenager in the 1955 American drama Rebel Without a Cause, there was an even more iconic rebel: Marlon Brando as The Wild One. In stark contrast to Dean's simple red windbreaker, Brando not only wore a leather jacket but also rode a motorcycle as he and his gang rolled into a small town and invaded Bleeker's, a local cafe, to terrorize, carouse, and otherwise frighten the locals.

At one point in the film, a girl asked Johnny, Brando's character, "What are you rebelling against, Johnny?" He coolly replied, "Whatcha got?"

It may well have been that very scene that inspired the title of Dean's movie two years later. Rebellion for the sake of rebellion has a long history—and I, as a teen, was not exempt from it.

My rebellion, however, was always half-hearted. I loved my parents, I was proud of them, and for the most part I agreed with them on all the important issues of life. And as I look back at my upbringing, I realize I really had no cause to rebel against their parenting.

The closest we ever came to disagreement was over their decision to send me to the private school in Kansas. They wanted me to go for the opportunities it would bring me later in life. I understood their reasoning, but I still didn't want to go. I liked the comforts and privileges of where I was.

Now I will not go so far as to say I ever embraced their decision, but I did seek to embrace it—like a dieter trying to enjoy his lightly steamed broccoli or baked tofu. I saw it as a challenge, as a test of manhood. But the underlying unhappiness at being there eventually turned me into a sullen, sophomoric monster.

My physique precluded me from adopting the tough dress and mannerisms of a hoodlum. I could never convincingly pull that off. So I did the next best thing: I became a pseudointellectual. I dressed the part, donning black clothes—black corduroys, black sweater, black striped button-down, black tie (school rules and all). I spent my free hours locked in my bedroom, listening to Pink Floyd and other ponderous bands, singing along off-key because of the headphones. (Eh, who am I kidding? I would have been off-key anyway, even without the headphones.)

I similarly took to writing poetry, maudlin stuff, filled with teenage angst. I wrote of worms, masks, and walls. At this point in my life, I wasn't reading Freud. And all the Sproul manuscripts had been read and reread to the point of exhaustion. Instead what you would more likely find stuffed into my back pocket was a copy of Sartre's *No Exit*—just to demonstrate my intellectual bona fides.

I found a girlfriend who joined me in my despair and disdain. We convinced ourselves that among the several billion other people on the planet, we alone were the only authentic humans, that every smile was a lie or the fruit of wretched ignorance. From our lofty perch, we looked down on the world. "Soulmates" might have described our relationship—or so I thought, that is, until she discovered the world of fashion, and suddenly our formerly shared sophistication was out of style.

Despite my recalcitrant attitude, there was never a time when I saw my father as an enemy. In fact, I continued to argue theology with my friends, the theology inculcated in me by my father. I was blessed to spend two hours every Sunday with my father's mentor, John Gerstner, as he came and taught at the church I was attending. My ideological convictions were never in jeopardy of changing but instead openly deepened. It was just that my demeanor was sour, my outlook skeptical. And I was still filled with pride—pride that I was beyond my peers, beyond the adults in my life, beyond everyone who didn't recognize the real truth that I knew: the truth that the world was a nasty place.

Because I still loved and admired my dad, I was excited when he stopped in Wichita on one of his speaking trips. He took me to dinner, but we did not discuss any movies. Nor did we discuss what I was reading at the time. Instead, we discussed what *he* was reading: me.

This time he didn't take my sullenness as a personal offense. He didn't berate me or lecture me. But he did teach me. He was able to read my attitude, my ennui, my cynicism. And he went right to the heart of it all. Without warning or introduction, as we waited for our meals, he asked me this simple yet direct question: "What are you rebelling against?"

Had I seen *The Wild One* by this point in my life, I surely would have echoed Brando's character with, "Whatcha got?" But I had yet to see the movie, and so I didn't know what to say. My deepest fears were coming to life right before my eyes: My father was peering into my soul. The veil had been lifted, and he wasn't excited about what he was seeing.

I hemmed and hawed a response, fidgeting while trying to rationally explain my irrational disdain for the world around me. He read me well enough to know that I was both frustrated and embarrassed. And then, knowing I was defeated, he spoke wisdom to me.

"Son," he said, "the quickest shortcut to developing a reputation as an intellectual is to adopt the posture of a cynic."

My father had an incomparable way of packing immense truth into so few words. And here, he had done it again. And it was always most jolting when the truth he proclaimed landed squarely on my own shoulders and not on someone else's.

His sagacious response shook me for several reasons. First, it was true. People often confuse cynicism for wisdom. Cynicism is reflected in that pedestrian expression, "Been there, done that, got the T-shirt." That little aphorism is a modern version of Solomon's complaint, "There is nothing new under the sun" (Ecclesiastes 1:9). World-weariness looks to others like worldly wisdom. Hope, trust—these are seen as childish qualities that we learn to leave behind as we experience the world.

The second reason his response so captured me was because it showed that he saw through my demeanor. My anemic answer to his probing question proved to him beyond any doubt what I was truly hungry for: to be respected for my intellect. I wanted others to think that the things that mattered to me mattered. I wanted my life and my thoughts to be objectively important. He acutely saw that I was aspiring to significance, something that I eventually learned *everyone* hungers for, to one degree or another.

The third reason his reply was so powerful was because it showed he knew just how to motivate me in a loving way. In that crucial moment, when he could have rightly crushed me under the weight of my own sin, he instead chose a path that would help me to see how I had been deceiving myself. He didn't shame me for the pride inherent in my posture. He didn't laugh at my presumption. Instead he appealed to something he already knew was in me: a desire to be genuine and to earn what I have. He was telling me not only would my shortcut not get me to where I wanted to go but also that it was cheating to venture down the path I had chosen.

This too shifted how I saw my father. I came to grasp that, for all his fame, for all his accolades, there were people out there—like the "pastor" who told him he was a fool for believing in the resurrection of Christ—who saw my father as a country bumpkin, naive, easily duped. And he just flat didn't care. He didn't devote his life to making sure others thought him sophisticated and urbane. He instead devoted his life to serving the Lord Jesus Christ through the gifts the Lord gave him.

My father was both brilliant and profoundly wise. He was able to expose the folly of the world with simple logic. He was, to the secular regime, the little boy who, without the least affectation, pointed out that the emperor had on no clothes. At first the people laughed at that boy and mocked him. But none of that changed the simple and objective truth, that the only suit the emperor had on was his birthday suit. To be able to do that, you have to know where you stand—and it better not be on the faux foundation of respectability but on the unshakable rock of the Rock.

The world tells us that everything we see was not—and then suddenly was. It exploded, naturalistic materialists tell us, into being by random, purposeless chance. My father was wont to ask two simple questions in reply.

First, what is "it"?

And second, what power does chance have?

The universe can't explode into being, because *it* isn't there to explode. Nonbeing isn't a prison from which the universe escaped. It. Is. Nothing.

And *chance*—that isn't even a veritable thing. It is instead a word we use to describe odds. But chance has no power, because it, like the universe before it, has no being. Suggesting the cosmos sprang from itself is about as plausible and respectable as someone telling you he wasn't born of his parents but that he unintentionally created himself from nothing.

This, however, doesn't merely answer the folly of the fool, but it reveals the glory of wisdom.

You can't be cynical about the creation—about the glory of God revealed in His spoken Word, about His power that called forth from nothingness countless billions of galaxies.

You can't be cynical about the incarnation—about God Himself taking on flesh and dwelling among us.

You can't be cynical about the cross—about the Father pouring out the wrath due to us on His own beloved Son instead.

You can't be cynical about the resurrection—about the yawning hole where the stone had once been, the angel announcing, "Why do you look for the living amidst the dead?"

You can't be cynical about the ascension of Christ—about His receiving the seat of power and authority over all things.

If we merely assent intellectually that these are propositional truths, but we don't see the glory in them, then we are no better than the demons who believe and tremble (James 2:19). If we taste boredom in the midst of the theater of His glory—in the midst of the story of Jesus Christ, the Second Adam, bringing all things under subjection—then we are monkeys with our eyes, ears, and mouths covered: See no glory, hear no glory, speak no glory.

Whatcha Got?

We are not supposed to be world-weary, but rather excited about His world, like children on Christmas morning. We are supposed to look up at the night sky and see it for what it is, a glorious and harmonious dance, a dazzling display of celestial fireworks. And we are supposed to squeal with delight to our heavenly Father, "Do it again, Daddy!"

If we are to see the kingdom of God, we must be like children. We must have the courage to stand before a world that can't be bothered to care—and care. While they scoff at us, mock us, rage against us, we must still embrace the impertinence of being earnest.

It is possible—indeed, it is not too terribly difficult—to fool the world of fools. We can pose as cynics, dress ourselves as skeptics, and maybe even receive a begrudging nod of respect from the world. If, however, we act embarrassed of our heavenly Father, He warns us that on the Day of Judgment, He will act embarrassed of us. Which would you rather have, my father was asking me that day: the miserly respect of the world, or the prodigal love and delight of your heavenly Father?

My departure from pseudo-intellectualism was not immediate. The process was a transformation that took some time. I continued to write poetry, none of it terribly earnest, but my outlook changed. I moved from dark and ponderous to light and playful. That day my father had shown me the way out; he had opened the door for me. And he encouraged me, in that I knew he had walked out on that same path. He taught me that day to start chipping away at the idol I had been dragging along through my days like a fool—my pride.

My heavenly Father has done still more, leaving me room to utterly destroy my reputation, that I would learn more fully that my only boast is in Christ. And all the while, both of my fathers—my earthly father and my heavenly Father—have walked with me and loved me faithfully.

I have far too much to believe in to ever become skeptical. Let the world laugh in its mockery, as long as Christ calls me His and laughs with me in our shared joy. I have much to embrace, much to rejoice in, much to marvel over, much to give thanks for. It turns out that, contrary to popular belief, "nothing" isn't what sleeping rocks dream of. Nor is it what I did all day in the ninth grade. It is, instead, what I have to rebel against.

12

Santini!

I noted earlier that my father was a Renaissance man, gifted in myriad ways. What I have not mentioned yet was that he was a highly proficient ping-pong player. He learned to play from Dr. Bill Walk, his high school friend who went on to coach the United States National Table Tennis Team, which traveled to play the Chinese national team during Nixon's efforts at détente with communist China. (The visit worked wonders. *Time* magazine called it "the ping heard 'round the world.")

I also noted earlier that my father, in addition to the scores of theology books he had penned, wrote a novel, *Johnny Come Home*. What I didn't mention was that although the novel did not sell well, it was quite good. If you think I'm prejudiced in my assessment—okay, guilty as charged—don't just take my word for it. Elisabeth Elliot called it "a page-turner," and I couldn't agree more. Although it was a work of "fiction," it was great fun to guess who inspired each character and which of the stories were borrowed from my father's actual past.

Through a mutual friend, the manuscript was passed along to Pat Conroy, a favorite author of both my father and me. Conroy was the author of *The Water Is Wide*, which was adapted into the film

Conrack, as well as the novels *The Lords of Discipline*, *The Prince of Tides*, and *The Great Santini*. Conroy loved *Johnny Come Home* and graciously provided an endorsement for the back cover.

My father and I returned the favor by loving Conroy's works. When I was seeking a master's degree in English, my thesis was on his works. Conroy's novels had the same peculiar relationship to history that my father's novel did. They all have, in the first page or two, a disclaimer that was no doubt written by some lawyer, claiming that what we're about to read is a work of fiction and that the characters in the story are not meant to represent anyone. But if you know anything about the life of the author, you soon come to realize that that legalese is pure blarney.

Conroy and ping-pong come together in my memory when I'm on the tennis court. I didn't start playing tennis in earnest until I was in high school, but even then, *mediocre* is the kindest term any impartial observer could honestly say about my game, despite my devoting countless hours to mastering it.

My father, on the other hand, never played tennis. I remember when I was in the fourth grade, my father asked me which sport I enjoyed playing the most. He was surprised when I answered, "Soccer," a sport that, at that time, precious few American nine-year-olds had even played. Although I was but nine, he gave me a little peek into psychology when he said, "I suspect you like soccer so much because I never played it. It's an arena where you can excel that I haven't been a part of."

Returning now to Conroy. If you are not acquainted with *The Great Santini*, the film version starred Robert Duvall as Lt. Col. "Bull" Meechum, a brutal Marine pilot and alpha male of the Meechum family. The story is told from the perspective of his teenage son, Ben.

Santini!

Not coincidentally, Pat Conroy was raised by a fighter pilot who was as brutal as Duvall's character. The portrayal by Duvall created quite a rift in the Conroy family—which would be strange if he were simply a fictional character.

Bull was a bull, more drill sergeant than father, an egomaniac who seemed to delight in psychologically torturing his children. He was hypercompetitive, and when victory in a game was evident, he would beat his chest and bellow, "I am the great Santini!"

Part of what makes the story so moving are the conflicted feelings Ben has for his father. He respects his father, admires him, and yet, at the same time, despises him. He wants to be just like him—and nothing like him at all. The reader, or the viewer, comes away feeling the same. The climactic scene finds Ben telling his drunken father, who can't even stand up at this point, that he loves him. Bull rages, but the love keeps coming. (It's hard to not love Robert Duvall, whatever character he plays, but I digress.)

Another key moment in the story is a game of one-on-one basketball between father and son. The whole family watches as the son is about to defeat his father for the first time. The son delights in the moment and takes the opportunity to goad his father on. After the son scores the winning basket, the family rejoices, but Bull then changes the rules, insisting that now you must win by two points. The son refuses to cooperate, and Bull's rage grows.

If anyone thinks I am telling this story to suggest my relationship with my father was similar to the father-son relationship in the Meechum family, they would be grossly mistaken. My father was a kind and gracious man. Competitive, yes, just like me. But he took no pleasure in hurting anyone.

He did identify with the competitive nature of Bull Meechum, but that's where the parallels end. I noted earlier that my father would only play one-on-one with me up to three points—three points, because that's all his stamina would allow. He wanted to join me in my interests, but he also didn't want to lose.

When I took up tennis, my father, wanting to be involved in my life, took up tennis too. He wasn't so much interested in learning as in winning. And he certainly wasn't interested in having me teach him. I'd already proven to be a lousy coach.

One illustration will suffice. Just a few years before, I had taken him snow skiing for his first time. Somehow I coaxed him up to the top of the bunny slope, a gentle incline for novices and children alike. My instructions were simple: "If you want to turn to the left, point your right ski inward. If you want to turn to the right, point your left ski inward. If you want to stop, point them both inward." That was the sum total of the lesson I gave him. Needless to say, his day didn't end too well, and that proved to be the end of my giving him skiing lessons.

With respect to tennis, he had his own unique strategy. He had no interest in hitting any winners. He knew all he had to do to win was return the ball. He literally gripped his racket halfway up the arm. He played like it was ping-pong, and he was on defense, waiting for me to grow impatient and spike it out of bounds. He looked more like a hockey goalie than a tennis player, moving just enough from side to side to dink the ball back over the net.

The strategy I chose was to try to tire him out by forcing the ball to the edges—but in so doing, I only managed to tire myself out. More often than not, my attempts at landing the ball just inside bounds resulted in my hitting the ball just out of bounds, beyond the line. He was employing Muhammad Ali's rope-a-dope, taking everything I had until I was too tired to fight back.

More important, however, was his ability to get inside my head. In 1943, Pittsburgh Pirates pitcher Rip Sewell unveiled for the first time in forty years the Eephus pitch. Sometimes called a balloon ball or a parachute ball, the Eephus pitch arcs high and slow, at half the speed of a changeup and a third of the speed of a fastball. Sewell won twenty games that year, and throughout his career he gave up only one homerun with the Eephus, and that was to Ted Williams, in an All-Star game. While a normal changeup uses a shift in velocity to fool the batter, the Eephus added this element: the juiciness of the slow-moving ball. A batter would find his heart racing as he waited for the ball's arrival, only to find that he couldn't wait any longer, and then he would swing well ahead of the ball.

That's what my father gave me on the tennis court: the opportunity to set up whatever shot I wanted. But I could never wait. Anticipation turned to frustration. But my dad did not let up. With every unforced error I would make, he would hold his racquet aloft and shout, "Santini!" He would chatter at me throughout the match, teasing me, "I thought you played this game every day." And, "You are looking kind of tired." And after another ball into the net, "Frustrating, isn't it, son?"

As with Bull Meechum, his head games worked on me. Unlike Bull Meechum, though, there was nothing sinister in his game. He wasn't trying to be mean-spirited toward me. Even the allusions to Santini were just part of our life together, something we shared.

My father, as was so often the case, was trying to teach me something on the court, and it was this: Anything that is a strength can become a weakness, and anything that is a weakness can become a strength. When it came to sports, I had few gifts, except a strong will. That strong will could, however, and often did, become a liability as I would grow easily frustrated and therefore distracted. Conversely, my father's weakness—that he hadn't the faintest idea how to hit a topspin forehand, nor how to smoke a serve—became a strength in that I didn't know how to play with no pace on the ball.

A second lesson, however, had an even broader application. He was teaching me to separate my emotions from the task at hand. He was teaching me to focus. His practical lesson on the tennis court found expression not much later when he gave me a copy of *The Inner Game of Tennis*, a classic from 1974, before "sports psychology" was even a thing. The book explained how our inner-talk to ourselves on the tennis court is as much a challenge as the person on the other side of the net. We create self-doubt and prepare ourselves for failure. Though the book had its share of psychological mumbo jumbo, it also had application off the tennis court.

As a writer, for instance, my self-doubt typically runs along these lines: "I don't have enough to say." I wrote my first book as a very young man and felt like I had poured just about everything I knew into it. My next book came out a full fourteen years later, and again I felt like I had, in the two books, covered the gamut of what I knew.

So the blank page that stares at me when I sit down to write again mocks me, reminds me of my limited knowledge, reminds me of the negative reviews I've read. That insecurity, however, can become a strength, as it drives me not to fluff up what I'm writing to fill the page but to be sure I'm not wasting a word. As aspiring writers are always told, "Kill your darlings." Stephen King said it most powerfully: "Kill your darlings, kill your darlings, even when it breaks your egocentric little scribbler's heart, kill your darlings."

It is critical, likewise, when I'm seeking to persuade someone, that my desire to win the argument not lead me away from winning the person. When *ad hominems* begin to fly, the wise man keeps his eye on the ball. He doesn't descend into the muck, nor does he forget that the person on the other side of the argument is a person.

My father was a brilliant man, and a passionate one. What he was teaching me was the importance, at one and the same time, of keeping brilliance and passion together and of keeping them separate. We rightly keep the two together when the things we know don't just stay in our minds but move into our hearts. We rightly separate them when we don't allow our passion to cloud our thinking.

Between the two of us, I was clearly the superior tennis player. He, however, was the master of self-control. He was likewise the master of getting me off my game—which is why he always won. Every time we played.

To this day, every time the wind blows I hear his voice saying, "I am the great SANTINI!"

13

Angels Dancing on My Pinhead

It would be a gross error to conclude that, because my father was such a gifted theologian, he must have led a peculiarly strict and pious household. It would be equally incorrect to conclude that all theologians' kids are kissin' cousins of PKs (pastors' kids) and thus share in their presumed stereotypical propensity for raw and outright rebellion. Neither of those extremes would describe the home in which I was raised.

I have sought to belabor the fact that my parents, in their desire to raise my sister and me in the nurture and admonition of the Lord, did so not in a programmatic way but in an organic fashion. As a child, I was not required to memorize the Westminster Shorter Catechism or any other creed of the Christian faith. In fact my first experience with "family worship" was around the dinner table—at a friend's house.

There was one time, however, when a program found its way into our home.

When my sister and I were both in grade school, my father sat us down one evening after dinner and began to take us through the Bethel Series. Now more than fifty years old, the program is designed to give laypeople a basic understanding of the content, themes, and flow of the Bible. With forty lessons in total, each one is complete with an elaborate painting illustrating the main point of the lesson. I remember my father showing us the first picture, with its contrast of the glory of Eden and what lay to the east, its broken musical note, denoting the loss of harmony. I suspect I still remember that picture because, well, it was the *only* one I ever saw. That was the end of our experiment in programs. Perhaps my father's gift of explaining the complex to the simple wasn't quite honed enough to get through to me.

My parents did, of course, pray with me and for me. I was probably six when, for the first time, while my mother prayed with me during my bedtime, I asked Jesus into my heart. It would not, however, be the final time. For two weeks during the summers when I turned eight and nine, I attended Bible camp just outside Ligonier. There, like scores of other kids, I drank bug juice, woke to the sound of reveille, and walked the aisle committing my life to Christ.

By the time I was in high school, I had reached a few conclusions that did not help me sleep well at night. I had never doubted that God had made the world, that Jesus was His Son, or that the Bible was His Word, true and accurately preserved from beginning to end. As I grew older, however, I came to understand that if I wanted my sins to be forgiven, I would need to own the faith on my own and seek to put my sins behind me. As my interest in theology grew, I became even more convinced of those two truths: First, that the Bible was true; and second, that I was not yet fully committed to following Jesus.

Every Sunday I attended two adult Sunday schools in addition to the worship service. During the school week, I passed notes in my classes. Those notes, however, were not about which girl I had a crush on; instead they were theological arguments made against my not-yet-Reformed friends. I even became, in a manner of speaking, the leader of my own small cadre of likeminded students and evangelized in an effort to grow that group.

Each night, though, when I climbed into bed, I would look out my bedroom window at the stately oak tree in the back yard as the Kansas south wind would cause it to teeter back and forth precariously, thinking all the while to myself, *If that tree falls in my sleep and kills me, I will wake up in hell, with no chance to escape.* I did not hide my situation from my friends, and they prayed faithfully for me.

I did, however, hide it from my parents. There came a time when it was expected that I would join our local church, but not before making a profession of faith. I knew what to say. I even believed what I said. I just didn't believe that I really believed. I was welcomed into membership, and to the Lord's Table. I believed enough, however, to know that I should not take the bread and the wine while not believing. On communion Sundays I would sit apart from my parents, so they would not see me pass the elements along without partaking.

That nightly fear gnawed at me for months. I didn't sleep well. I thought about talking to my parents about it, but I didn't want to worry them. I thought it better to let them think the best of me. I now know I reached that conclusion for my own sake and not for theirs.

One evening I sat alone in my room listening to Bob Dylan. Not the esoteric-voice-of-his-generation Bob Dylan, but, rather, the evangelical-Christian Bob Dylan. It was his second album of that phase of his life, entitled simply *Saved*. As the needle flowed through its groove, as Dylan's nasally voice filled my ears, I realized how foolish I had been. I knew God had made me. I knew that Jesus was His Son. I knew everything I needed to know, and I knew it all to be true. What, I asked myself, was I waiting for? What sins that I was not prepared to give up were more valuable than peace with the living God?

I prayed there, on my knees, asking that God would forgive my sins, that His Spirit would indwell me, that He would lead me in paths of righteousness, that He would adopt me as His son. I wept in gratitude and, like John Bunyan's Christian, felt the great weight taken off my shoulders. I could have stayed there in that posture and setting of worship the rest of my life. But whatever chance there was of that happening was soon interrupted by my host mother calling me to dinner.

The school I attended, although private and exclusive, was not a boarding school. I stayed with a different family each of my two years. The first year my hosts were professing Christians. In fact, that's how I had come to own that Bob Dylan record. When at the record store with my host older brother, I had been too ashamed to buy more Pink Floyd. Christian Bob Dylan was the best compromise.

My second year I stayed with folks who were not Christians. I hoped, perhaps naïvely, that as I came to the dinner table, I might let off a Moses-down-from-the-mountain glow that might draw them in. No such luck. Or rather, no such providence.

Although it meant confessing to my parents that my profession of faith a year earlier had been bogus, I knew I had to tell them. I called them that night. Fighting through the tears, explaining to them that I had always believed that what they believed was true, that I had always desired that they would be proud of me, I told them that just that day I had embraced the work of Christ for me and surrendered my self-will.

Both of my parents listened patiently. They encouraged me to never fail to rejoice in my redemption. They encouraged me to seek the face of God all my days. They no doubt rejoiced that God's promise to Abraham—that his descendants would be as the stars in the sky—was fulfilled, that God was not just a God to them but also to their children. I expected them to be happy. What believing parent wouldn't be? And indeed they were.

What I didn't expect, however, were the last words my father left me with that night. Despite the study I had done, despite all that I had learned through the years, he obliquely referenced a text I had never before heard.

"Son, tonight the angels in heaven are rejoicing for your sake," he said.

My first reaction was pious and careful. I believe what I said was verging on the profound and thoughtful, something along the lines of, "Huh?"

With just the slightest hint of exasperation, he responded, "Check it out, in Luke 15."

After that phone call I returned to my room, picked up my Bible, and turned to Luke 15. There, Jesus gives three of His parables of the lost being found. The bulk of the chapter recounts the story of the prodigal son. Though I was certainly a sinner and had gone off from Pennsylvania to the distant lands of Kansas, I hoped my parents did not see me as that son. The first parable in the chapter was the parable of the lost sheep, the ninety-nine and the one. Sandwiched in between those parables is the parable of the lost coin. Jesus, in all three of the parables, notes that the stories end with a party, a celebration.

In the lost coin parable, however, it is not just the woman who lost the coin who celebrated; it was the angels. The parable ends, "Likewise, I say to you, there is joy in the presence of the angels of God over one sinner who repents" (Luke 15:10).

Within hours of coming into the kingdom, I was taught what may well be the single most important lesson there is about living in the kingdom—that the kingdom does not exist for the sake of its citizens but for the sake of its King. The angels' joy for me was and is, I'm sure, genuine. Because they are without sin, they surely must love all those their Maker loves. I was not beloved of the Father because I came to faith. Rather, I was brought to faith because I was beloved of the Father.

The center of the angels' celebration, however, was not me but the One who had rescued me. They were celebrating the glory of the work of Christ, the potency of the work of the Spirit, and the tenderness and beauty of the Father's plan.

One could argue that this, my final conversion experience, was the least credible of them all. I've already confessed my nightly fears of death and damnation. Wasn't this just fire insurance, a desperate ploy to placate the wrath of the Father against me? Fear of judgment seems a rather selfish motive for embracing the work of Christ, doesn't it?

The truth, however, is that Jesus Himself wasn't averse to warning of the wrath to come, to calling all men everywhere to repent, lest they be left outside the gates where there is weeping and gnashing of teeth. Jesus spoke of hell, of final punishment for the finally impenitent, more than everyone else in the whole Bible combined. When He did so, however, He wasn't taking a fiendish delight in scaring people. Instead, He spoke truth in love, forewarning His hearers about the reality that lies ahead. And, like a mother hen who longs to bring wayward chicks under her wings, He wept over the lost (Luke 19).

What my father's last reminder did was turn my gaze away from my rescue and draw it toward my Rescuer. He was telling me that the true glory of the gospel was not that I had escaped hell but that Jesus, the express image of the Father's glory, was glorified in dying for me and for all those He came to save. This, in turn, reminded me that not only is heaven not all about me, but neither is the church. Because He had given me faith, I was joining the chorus of the angels and the souls of other justified men made perfect in ascribing glory to the Second Adam.

My father was telling me this, as well, in his own words: that the kingdom of heaven is not just a party but the true mother of all parties. It is not just a place of joy but the dwelling place of true Joy, whom we know to be Jesus.

And he was preparing me for this day, when he and I would be separated—when he would be united fully with his Redeemer. My father is at that party, and one day, the day my heavenly Father has appointed, I will join him there. Better still, I will join Him there.

14

Those Angry Young Men and Their Haughty Cacophonies

I find some comfort in the fact that I'm not alone in my folly. Jesus warned us against it, telling us time and again that a servant is not greater than the Master, that we should expect trouble and tribulation. With each generation, however, we think we've glommed onto this great new strategy—what if we could make Christianity cool?

We see it in our day in millennials adopting hipster styles and politically-correct social causes. We saw it a generation ago in the late sixties and early seventies as "the Jesus People" sought to meld together the sensibilities of hippies and Christians.

My first venture into this folly happened while I was at Bible camp. I was nine years old that summer. Each session of camp, campers were called upon to take up the tasks of the counselors. I was chosen by my cabin to be counselor for the day. This meant I would have to lead the devotional that evening.

It was my very first public speaking engagement, there in a tiny cabin in the dark. My brilliant idea was to present a case for both creation and evolution. I was blazing a path, leading my cabin mates to the Promised Land where you could, at one and the same time, believe the Bible and still be thought sophisticated by the world.

I succeeded about as well those who continue to blaze that trail today. That is to say, I failed miserably. We seem think we can walk through Gettysburg in grey pants and a blue coat and not get shot at. Instead, we get shot at by both sides.

Having professed faith in Christ once again, and for the last time, in high school, I still had to relearn that lesson. For many young Christians that pathway involves embracing the bride of Christ but then mocking her when surrounded by unbelieving friends, by enemies of Christ. We beat the unbeliever to the punch when we quote approvingly the words of Gandhi, who said, "I like your Christ. I do not like your Christians. Your Christians are so unlike your Christ."[6]

Gandhi, of course, is quite right that we Christians are so unlike our Christ. That's kind of the point, isn't it? Christianity isn't about our following Him but about His rescuing us. To be sure, we are called to grow in likeness to Him. When we do, however, we should find ourselves loving His bride, the church, as He does. It is precisely because we are not like Christ that Christ came—to be us in the eyes of the Father, on the cross.

When you are well trained theologically, it is especially easy to look down your nose at the church. When you have answers to questions that other Christians haven't even considered, the devil is right at your doorstep, encouraging his favorite sin—pride. And I was no exception.

I took it upon myself to begin reading the best and the brightest in the church. I remember reading—no, devouring—Francis Schaeffer's *A Christian Manifesto* while flying home from the

Those Angry Young Men and Their Haughty Cacophonies

Congress on the Bible in San Diego. I read Augustine's *Confessions*. I read Luther's brilliant, albeit caustic, *The Bondage of the Will*, in response to Erasmus' *On the Freedom of the Will*.

As my father continued to write, I continued to read. And while his arguments followed the same pattern of others' whom I had read, his arguments had a spirit of peace.

And I didn't care for it.

I was drawn more toward Schaeffer's scathing critique of the broader culture and toward Luther's snarky retorts to Erasmus. I was redeemed, forgiven, adopted—but I was still an angry young man.

My father's interest in my education and his concern over my angry disposition converged one afternoon when I was seventeen. He asked, as was his habit, what I had been reading of late. I was excited to let him know. I had discovered a new writer—young, well-trained, with a good pedigree, and with a vibrant style. I had been reading *Addicted to Mediocrity* by Franky Schaeffer. Franky, now Frank, is the son of Francis Schaeffer and the producer of their dramatic series on the decay of ethics in America, *Whatever Happened to the Human Race?*

In *Addicted to Mediocrity*, Franky took on the baleful state of evangelical aesthetics. He mocked our propensity for preachy, heavy-handed, message-based art; our love of kitschy, lowbrow trinketry; our embrace of all manner of "Jesus junk."

And I ate it up.

As I look back, there was something Jekyll and Hyde about my love for the book. His book rightly affirmed the glorious Reformational truth that the Lordship of Christ touches on every part of reality, that the call to exercise dominion over creation abides with us, even after the fall, that Jesus does indeed change everything. That was good. And it was good that I liked it, learned from it, and was inspired by it.

The Hyde part was the fiendish delight I took in his swipes at my more "pedestrian" evangelical brethren.

When my father heard what I was reading, he didn't take time to praise either Franky or me for the good things in his work, but instead once more peered right into my still darkened soul and warned me unequivocally.

"Be careful, Son," he said. "He is an angry young man."

At the moment, that comment didn't have too great an impact on me. In fact, I probably once more had a Jekyll and Hyde response. The Jekyll part of me remembered that my father was a wise man—that he knew me, that he knew which side of any given horse I was more apt to fall off. I briefly acknowledged this, put it in my pocket, and filed it away to contemplate another day.

My Hyde response was easy enough to predict. I thought my dad was a mite soft, that he needed to drink a bit of the heady concoction known as righteous indignation. Franky was angry, and so was I. And didn't we have reason to be? Shouldn't the church's wholesale abandonment of high art raise our collective ire? Shouldn't we embrace the bombast of Luther and nail our ninety-five theses to the door of a glowing Kinkade cottage?

Franky's anger was a cannon, and it needed to be fired.

A few years later I read two more of young Mr. Schaeffer's efforts: *A Time for Anger* and *Sham Pearls for Real Swine*. I also took the occasion to watch Franky's first and only Hollywood film, *Wired to Kill*.

What I noticed in the books was that Franky's musical tastes weren't as developed as one might expect they would be, as he seemed to play only one melody: "Evangelicals are rubes! Evangelicals are hayseeds! Evangelicals are jejune!"

Those Angry Young Men and Their Haughty Cacophonies

There was no new insight in the latter books that had not been in the first, but there was a whole new heaping pile of anger. Franky's cannon was firing on rubble he had already created. I began to suspect that perhaps my dad might have had a very good point.

The last book I read of Franky's—though by then he was just Frank—was his novel *Portofino*. He clearly lifted pages from my father and from Pat Conroy, in that the characters in the book, if you knew anything of the author's life, were readily identifiable. And those characters came out smelling like a rose that had been left a month ago in a pile of manure.

The evangelical world was all in a tizzy, because Franky was goring the sacred cows that his parents had become. How, we all wondered, could Franky do such a thing? Well, we didn't *all* wonder that. My wise father did not. It surprised him not at all.

I don't know how life was in the Schaeffer home when Franky was growing up. I do know that in the evangelical world, we tend to swing between the pendulums of hagiography and slander, either exalting our heroes or casting them out as unworthy. Franky's earlier works had helped me to see from which side Franky swung.

As my father had warned me, Franky was, proverbially speaking, a loose cannon. When that cannon, firing erratically, hit my enemies, I cheered it on. When it fired on the rubble it had created, I began to lose interest. But when it fired on my friends, I became a truly angry young man.

I tried to be understanding. I looked into my own life: the son of a well-respected, well-known theologian and apologist; the son of a man others tended to see as without fault or blemish. I hoped I could find understanding for what Franky had done.

But it didn't work.

Instead I came out of my Franky crush determined that whatever I might do, wherever I might end up, I would, by God's good grace, never dishonor my parents the way he had dishonored his. Indeed, along the way, when my sins have brought shame on my family name, I have been tempted to comfort myself this way: "At least I'm not Franky Schaeffer."

Since *Portofino*, Frank Schaeffer has continued not merely to drift slowly from his moorings but to flee them with all the zeal of Jonah. And he has made shipwreck of his faith. He has, in his old age, become a caricature of himself as a young man, angry at whatever comes before his fading eyes, using his cache as a former member of evangelical royalty to gain an audience, playing the fool.

Anger is a heady brew and, therefore, dangerous. It took some time, but in witnessing the fruit of Frank Schaeffer's bitter root, which my father diagnosed long before it blossomed, I learned a great deal about grace. I learned that one cannot love Christ while hating His bride, those whom He loves, those for whom He died. I've learned that I am called to see my fellow believers with the eyes of Him in whom we believe. Our heavenly Father looks at every believer and sees there every perfection of His glorious Son, imputed to them.

More powerfully still I have now lived long enough to know how vital it is for others to see me the way my heavenly Father sees me. Like Ham exposing his father's nakedness, so too did Frank expose his own nakedness. And like a prodigal son, I have had my own nakedness exposed. Which is why I need to be covered—not by the animal skin that Shem and Japheth placed on their father, but by the blood of the perfect Lamb, placed on me by my heavenly Father.

There is such a thing as righteous anger. I would never deny that. More often than not, however, we pan for the fool's gold that is nothing more than self-righteous anger. Pride digs in deep, and its noxious weeds crop up all over the garden we've been called to guard. My father warned me about reading young Franky Schaeffer, not because he was concerned with Franky Schaeffer but because he was worried about me. His insight into Franky was deep. His insight into me was even deeper.

My father was not a perfect man. I don't want this collection of memories to descend into a false, airbrushed portrait of the man. I want it to be true, and I want it to be beautiful, because, by His grace, my father was a good man. He, like my heavenly Father, was patient with me. Like my heavenly Father he led me into greater wisdom. Like my heavenly Father he worked to put to death my pride and, with it, my anger, that I might bear the fruit of the Spirit—love, joy, peace, patience, kindness, goodness, faithfulness, gentleness, and self-control (Galatians 5:22–23).

15

Mice on the Doorstep

The man who started the private school I attended in high school was a devoted Christian named Robert D. Love. His motives for starting that school, however, were born out of a different ideological commitment than what you might think. He took issue with public schools, not so much because they espoused left-wing ideology, nor even because they banished the Bible, public prayers, and Christian morals. Instead, his grave concern was that public schools were run by the government. Mr. Love, you see, was a true libertarian, before being libertarian was cool.

An oft-repeated story was that three years after the school opened, a gentleman from the state board of education showed up, asking for the school's "papers." The biggest problem with this request was that Mr. Love had not obtained permission from the state to start the school. In fact, he hadn't even bothered to mention to the state that the school existed. And he wanted no part of signing their "papers."

In response to the request from the state's educational representative, Mr. Love offered this challenge: "Pick any class from any school in the state. We'll bring our corresponding class to wherever that is. Give both classes the same test, any test. If your students outperform our students, then we'll talk about signing your papers."

With that, the gentleman from the state left, never to return.

Mr. Love's interest in theology caused his path to cross with my father's. And that, in a nutshell, is how I ended up in Kansas. Mr. Love, however, was more of a prophet than a student. He learned much from my father but also taught my father quite a bit about free market economics and limited government. And he, along with his irascible wife, Lil, taught me the same.

By the time I had finished my junior year at the school, I was a full-throated ideologue. My passions were twofold: Reformed theology and the Austrian school of economics. The latter, needless to say, ended up throwing a bit of a monkey wrench into my parents' plans for my education.

As my second year was drawing to a close, I asked my parents if I might apply to Grove City College instead of the Ivy League schools to which my parents hoped I might apply. Grove City College was known around the world for its commitment to Austrian economics, and only slightly less well known for the commitment of its Bible faculty to Reformed theology. My parents agreed. I applied and was accepted.

I was a rather naive freshman. I assumed that not only would every member of the faculty share my zeal and ideological commitments but that the entire student body would as well. Why else would anyone go to Grove City College? Well, it turns out that Grove City College turned out good students, at a relatively low price, and that those two features drew any number of students. It was also the case that there were plenty of faculty who were grateful to have jobs teaching and who actively sought to undermine the Christian faith and limited government.

And that was something that I felt compelled to change. At the same time, I feared that my father might be disappointed in my decision to attend Grove City College. The educational plan he had laid out for me seemed to be so important to him. I almost thought of him like the proverbial proud mother who longed to tell her friends about, "My son, at Princeton . . ."

For most of my life, my single greatest earthly fear was that I might disappoint my father. I looked up to him so much that all I wanted was to make him proud. But more often than not, my efforts failed, not because he was hard to please, but because I seemed to have a special gift for messing things up.

I didn't, as a student, go to class as much as I went to battle. I wanted to take on my professors and expose the flaws in their thinking. Now, you are probably thinking, "What an arrogant, prideful young man you must have been." And you'd be right on. But my father was more interested in teaching me humility than he was in teaching me ideology.

Several times a week I would call home from the payphone in my dorm hall. I would get my dad on the phone, and just as he would give my mother a shot-by-shot account of his golf game, I would give him a blow-by-blow recounting of my battles in class that week.

For example: There was an English professor who was particularly averse to my sundry ideologies. He seemed to think it was his calling to burst the bubbles of naiveté found in so many of the young Christian students at the college. As a result, he drew to himself, every year, a cadre of the disaffected—young men and women who saw him as a kind of guru. He was, in short, either loved or hated.

One day we were having a discussion on the American writer and Nobel Prize laureate William Faulkner. In Faulkner's novel *The*

Sound and the Fury, we are given a glimpse into how several different characters see the same events differently. The professor took the occasion to praise uncertainty and to laud a relativistic approach to reality. He gave a brief soliloquy that ended with the rhetorical question, "What is truth?"

Impertinently, I raised my hand.

"Yes, Mr. Sproul?" he asked.

"I am," I replied.

"You are *what?*" he retorted.

"You asked what is truth," I said. "The answer is 'I am.'"

He was annoyed at my simplicity, which is just what I was hoping for.

"You could be a figment of my imagination," he said. "I could be dreaming. There is no possible way for me to know that you are."

"That may be," I replied, "but *I* can know that *I* am. And *you* can know that *you* are. For you to be able to doubt your own existence, you would first have *to be*, wouldn't you? Think of Descartes' *Cogito, ergo sum*—'I think, therefore I am.' We can, in fact, know truth. Along the same lines, to say, 'We cannot know truth' is itself a truth claim."

The professor sighed, unimpressed. The bell rang, and class was dismissed.

It wasn't, however, just my ideological opponents with whom I went to battle. Even my friends—the professors I looked up to—were given much the same treatment. If there were some esoteric detail of my worldview that didn't match that of my professors, I would steer the conversation to that point and then go to war. Even "my guy," Dr. Andy Hoffecker—that one professor who was a guru to me—had the misfortune of having to deal with me as I turned every class into a debate on apologetic theory.

Mice on the Doorstep

These arguments were the first of what I like to call "dead mice on the doorstep."

If you've ever had an outdoor cat—which, in my opinion, is the only way to have a cat—you know what I'm referring to. For all their infamous disdain and aloofness, cats really do crave the approval of humans. That's why they put their prey on our doorsteps. They are saying in essence, "Look what I've done for you. Look at how I kept the house safe."

While my father was writing books, speaking at conferences, teaching on the radio, I was having arguments in class. While he was actually winning people to our shared convictions, I was merely annoying people. And worse, I was proudly reporting to him, looking for his approval for every little annoyance of which I was guilty. I was a cat blithely dropping dead mice on his doorstep.

How patiently he tried to help me. First he would simply remind me of my place. He would explain that I wasn't at Grove City College to teach but to learn, that even an utterly off-base professor could give me something worth holding on to. He, after all, had spent three years in seminary learning from men who didn't believe Jesus had been raised from the dead.

When that didn't seem to penetrate my thinking, he tried to get more practical. Although he didn't call it "Patriarchal Principle #2," he did intone the words with great solemnity.

"Son," he said pointedly, "never argue with a man holding a microphone."

That solemnity slowed me down, made me think, forced me to consider if perhaps he might be right. He went on to explain that it wasn't a fair fight, since the microphone was the most powerful weapon of all.

"The man with the microphone can shut you up, ignore you, insult you, do everything but answer the objection," he said, "and still come out looking to everyone like the winner. It doesn't help your cause, but it hurts it. Lay low, take notes, and if you must speak, ask questions. Not accusations disguised as questions, but genuine questions. That way you may help him."

There were a few occasions, here and there, where my father was present to witness my folly. That led him to drop more gems of wisdom on me. He watched me in battle, saw the fire in my eyes, heard the disgust in my voice, and thankfully, wasn't proud of what he saw.

"You seem to think that the goal is to win the argument," he said. "Don't you understand that the goal is to win the person?"

It was his version of that old nugget from Benjamin Franklin: "A man convinced against his will is of the same opinion still."

My father was a profoundly gentle man. About the only thing that was apt to raise his ire was seeing the weak be mistreated. And he was able to see that we all, in one way or another, are the weak. Often, even the bullies are weak, in an unseen way.

My father was also wont to say, "Scratch anger, and you are almost certain to find hurt." My mother was the same. When I went to her, with my ego bruised by someone teasing me for one thing or another, she would call on me to feel compassion, to see in the attacks I was receiving the pain of the one attacking.

The temper that my father labored to temper, the pride that he sought to put to death in me, are still there—part and parcel of the old man, the flesh, that still haunts me. My natural inclination is to see disagreement as a moral issue—to think that others aren't just wrong but wicked. Of course I judge myself far more graciously. And I also see disagreement as a lack of respect for me. It is an offense because I, like most people, operate under the unspoken assumption that I am somehow due respect. When I don't get it, I feel cheated, and I lash out.

All of this ought to be more than enough to humble me. And if not, there's still a seemingly unending list of sins that disqualify me from pride. What my father was trying to teach me was grace. He has been so often praised for his mental acuity, for his communication skills. But the truth of the matter is, he found his audience in large part because he was always so winsome. He was a charmer. Not in a dishonest way; he wasn't given to flattery. Rather, he managed to communicate, even over the radio while teaching millions of strangers, that he was for them.

And he was for me.

All that effort—all those putrid dead mice—was so utterly misguided. Not just because I mistreated the people I was arguing with, but because I misunderstood why my father loved me. He loved me because I was his son. No accomplishment, and no failure, would move the needle. I was his son, and that was more than enough.

Of course, the same is true of my heavenly Father. All my efforts to win His favor are ultimately an insult to His grace. He doesn't love me because of what I do but in spite of what I do. He loves me because of what His Son did for me. My calling is simply to rest. Yes, I am to strive to grow in grace, obedience, wisdom. And yes, the apostle Paul tells us to work out our salvation with fear and trembling (Philippians 2:12). But my work grows out of my rest, not the other way around.

No more dead mice on the doorstep. Just the risen Lamb.

16

Treasure Without a Map

It was perhaps the most public peek inside that many had ever had. Seeing my father ride along the corridors on a scooter, noting that he preached from a chair, witnessing the oxygen tank at his side—these were all obvious clues that my father's health was, let's just say, not as robust as it had once been.

There is, however, a difference between lacking robust health and being at death's door. That day, at our annual national conference, as my father took the stage to speak on the holiness of God, it seemed to many that the Grim Reaper must have been lurking impatiently in the wings.

I was there, and what I remember most was the faces of the watching congregants as they walked out of the sanctuary in tears—not because they had been confronted with God's holiness necessarily but because they had been deeply impacted by my father's frailty. He managed to make it through his abbreviated talk, and then he went to receive treatment. He was scheduled to speak first thing the next morning, but few expected to see him.

My father's days, however, were numbered by the living God. As the sun rose that next morning, so too did my father. He went to the pulpit and delivered an absolute tour-de-force lecture on secular worldviews. He was strong, cogent, insightful, engaging, and devastating to every thought that was raised against the Lordship of Christ.

My own response was a real roller-coaster ride. First I was shocked and overjoyed at his recovery. Then I was shocked and miffed that he had been able to take the information I had labored over for months in writing my book *Tearing Down Strongholds* and turn it into a single compelling address.

Then the obvious truth dawned on me: He hadn't stolen from me; he had invested in me. That book came out of me because he had put it in me. It was his to begin with. He had done so, however, so organically, that I couldn't trace the specific origins of any given thought.

What I've done thus far in this remembrance of his investment in me is to recollect not just the wisdom he gave me but also the circumstances in which he gave them, usually those circumstances being yet another example of my own folly. Some of the things I learned from him I know I will never forget, although I have forgotten when and where I first heard them. Some of them, I'm quite confident, you have heard as well.

My father attended graduate school at the Free University of Amsterdam. He went there to acquire a doctorate at the insistence of his mentor, Dr. John Gerstner. The Free University, founded by Abraham Kuyper, was the home of Dr. G. C. Berkouwer, the most prominent evangelical theologian in a doctoral program anywhere in the world. My father knew not a lick of the Dutch language. He opened his first book, looked up the first word in a Dutch-English dictionary, and wrote down on an index card the Dutch word on one side, the English on the other. Then he went to the second word and did the same. That was his method.

That, however, was not all he wrote on index cards. He also wrote these words and put the card before him on his desk as a constant reminder:

> *Your duty is to preach what the text says,*
> *not what you want it to say.*

I never saw that card, spending my family's sojourn in Holland in my mother's womb. But I did witness the fruit of that commitment.

My father recognized his calling to be in submission to the Word of God. It is so easy, when you're a student of the Bible, to begin to think that you are above God's Word, analyzing it. The truth is just the opposite. The proper, biblical perspective, however, is to remember that the Bible studies you. It is a mirror, James tells us, showing us what we are. It is not a tool that we use to persuade others to believe what we believe. Rather, it is God's tool to get us to believe what He knows.

And this is why I have never forgotten this nugget. My father delighted in highlighting the astonishing scope of the Bible. It is a book that not only shows us ourselves but reveals the infinite God. Every word is profitable, Paul tells us—which can create a temptation. How easy it is, when we're confronted with a text we either have difficulty understanding or difficulty submitting to, to move on to the next text. It's *all* good, after all. It's an endless buffet. And what could possibly be wrong in moving past one delicacy to dig into another?

My father, however, wisely said this: When you find yourself struggling with a text, do not simply move on to another. Chances are, if you are struggling with a text, it is because you need to wrestle with it. When the Bible puzzles us or rubs us the wrong way, we need to remember that it is right—and we are wrong. Where it confuses us is precisely the spot where we need to be corrected, reproved, instructed.

This truth has proven to be helpful to me over the years. My father was right. That itch, that twinge of discomfort we feel at certain texts—that's the radar letting us know there is something wrong in our perspective. It tells us we need to adjust our thinking, our doing, and that there is a thought not yet taken captive to the Lordship of Christ.

The more time we spend actually going through the Word—and not just going back to our favorite spots—the more apt we are to run into those rough patches. The Bible tells us that it is living and active. It is not just a repository of information; it is a sword, a sword that not only cuts us but excises from us our blots and blemishes.

My own tradition, the Reformed tradition, has its own share of weaknesses. When Paul warned that knowledge can puff up, I'm pretty sure he was talking to my tribe—and to me specifically. Our reputation as the most prideful bunch in all of Christendom is rather ironic, considering that we are the ones whose core doctrines begin with the total depravity of man. We believe that all men in their natural state not only need to be saved but cannot even call out to God to be saved unless God comes and changes them first. We believe that when the Bible says we are dead in our trespasses and sins, it means we are really and truly dead.

Why then would we be given to pride?

Because we're right. And that works in two directions. First, we're proud of being right. Second, we really are totally depraved—so depraved, in fact, that we can react to our affirmation of total depravity with pride rather than humility. What we do is take the Bible's description of us and our sin and turn it into a doctrine, a description of the problem of mankind.

But the Bible is not giving us anthropology. It is telling *me* what I am. It's talking to *me*.

I confess that I never actually heard this next nugget, which makes the above point quite well, directly from my father's lips. I heard instead about where it can be heard. There are a number of legends, true ones in fact, about how my father has crossed over into pop culture. It is true that he once played golf with Vince Furnier, known to the world as Alice Cooper. It is true as well that Gary Cherone, third lead singer for the band Van Halen, thanked my father for his influence in the liner notes of a Van Halen album.

The strangest appearance, however, is in an obscure art film from Abel Ferrara called *The Addiction*. Released to almost no acclaim or notice in 1995, the film is a vampire story, starring none other than Christopher Walken. In a climactic scene near the end, Casanova, the vampire that has seduced the protagonist into being a vampire says, "As R. C. Sproul says, 'We are not sinners because we sin. We sin because we are sinners.'"

Weird, huh?

As interesting a bit of pop culture trivia as that may be, the sentiment it contains is wisdom that has stuck with me. How easy is it to turn sin into something out there, something that happens to us, rather than recognizing it as something that flows out of us?

Just as I, as a boy, acted outraged and surprised with every dropped pop fly—when, in fact, I dropped them often—so too we act stunned when we, or others in our world, actually sin. In the church we all too often give lip service to the reality of sin but, like the Pharisees before us, labor to present ourselves as far better than we are. We cop to little sins—losing our tempers from time to time, showing some impatience, cheating on our diets. But we are—even born again, indwelt by the Spirit, declared righteous, and called saints by God Himself—far worse than that. We do things like deny the Lord, commit adultery and murder, show racial animosity.

We sin because we are, still, sinners.

We do, of course, make progress in our sanctification—what I like to call our "Jesus-ification." We are daily being made more and more like Him, as He washes us, His bride, with the water of His Word. When we get discouraged, it is important that we remember the progress we have been led through. When we get haughty, however, it is important that we remember how long a journey it is, from our rebirth to our full perfection. We may have traveled far, but glory is the last stop, and no, we are *not* almost there.

Which brings us to yet another nugget from my father. The Bible warns us against the danger of judging our righteousness against the righteousness of others. It warns us not just because doing so is wrong but because it is such an easy thing to fall into. Unbelievers, of course, are wont to think their eternal destiny is safe because they know people who are worse than they are. Hitler is a favorite stand-in for that role. Hell, to most unbelievers—if they are willing to affirm its existence at all—is a rather lonely place, occupied only by Hitler and any people in their lives who dared to judge them.

Believers, however, are susceptible to this same line of thinking. Paul warned the Corinthian believers against this temptation. We too want to judge ourselves by comparing ourselves to other believers. If, however, we want to understand what and who we are, we would judge ourselves not by the standards of other believers but by the standard of the One in whom we believe, Jesus.

My father used to say that if we were to create a spectrum of goodness, ranging from evil to godliness, with Adolf Hitler on one end and Jesus of Nazareth on the other, it is true enough that we would be between the two of them. That, however, is not much comfort when we realize we'd be standing right next to Hitler, with Jesus in another galaxy. We are far closer to Hitler than we are to Jesus, even we who aspire to be like Jesus.

That should put things in perspective. And as with so much of the rest of the things my father taught me, it ought to inform and to bolster our humility, our recognition of our dependence on the grace of God in Christ. It ought to put to death our deadly pride.

In God's grace, my father has finished his journey. His Jesus-ification is complete. And one day, when God so determines, mine too will be complete. Because the One who began a good work in us both will surely carry it through to the day of Christ Jesus.

17

Not a Piece of Chalk

I was blessed to be a student when Reformed Theological Seminary in Orlando first opened its doors. From my perspective, the school, although in its first year, had an all-star team for a faculty. I took classes with the inimitable Dr. Roger Nicole. I was led through the Old Testament by Dr. Richard Pratt Jr. I took classes from visiting faculty like Dr. John Gerstner and Dr. Carl Henry. Best of all, I took every class my father offered.

That ended up being quite a few classes. Because the faculty was being grown slowly, the early arrivals taught a broad range of classes. My clearest memory of that time was my oral final exam on an independent study I had done with my father during my final semester. He had assigned me the massive two-volume set of *Basic Writings of Saint Augustine*. He gave me my exam as our family drove together to my graduation ceremony at the original RTS campus in Jackson, Mississippi.

As I had read through the ponderous works of Augustine, I had developed a strategy to prepare for my final exam. I knew that Augustine was a deeply sound theologian, who occasionally nodded. (My father excused his failures by remarking, "Keep in mind,

Augustine didn't have an Augustine before him.") I figured that the only things I really needed to remember for the exam were those rare occasions when Augustine was wrong. Other than that, the correct answer to any question my father could throw at me about Augustine's theology was the correct answer in general. Easy-peasy.

Once again, my father outsmarted me. His exam went something like this.

"What was the first thing you read?" he asked.

I didn't remember. He allowed me to look at the table of contents.

"What did it say?" he asked.

I exposited on the theme for a few minutes then grew quiet.

"What else?" he asked.

I squeaked out a few more paltry thoughts, only to be met with yet another, "What else?" They just kept coming until I gave up. Then he asked, "What was the second thing you read?"

We went through the entire two volumes that way. My only comfort was the knowledge that I was on my way to my graduation, but it did teach a valuable lesson.

It was in our Introduction to Philosophy class my first semester, however, that he said something that truly gripped me. We were assigned to read *Thales to Dewey* by the great Christian philosopher Gordon Clark. He also assigned me, and only me, Clark's *A Christian View of Men and Things*.

On this particular evening, my father was explaining to us the distinctions between these three terms: paradox, contradiction, and mystery.

A paradox is something that sounds like a contradiction, but upon further examination, proves not to be. When Jesus says, "The first shall be last," He is speaking in paradox.

A mystery is something we do not yet understand. The origin of evil would fall into this category.

A contradiction is like a paradox in that it sounds like both sides of what it is saying cannot equally be true. It is like a mystery in that it is something we don't understand. But it is distinct from both. It is distinct from a paradox because it really is a contradiction; both sides cannot be true. And it is distinct from a mystery in that not only is it not understood but it absolutely *cannot* be understood, because it's nonsense.

Then, without telling us what he was doing, my father illustrated a contradiction for us. He held up a piece of chalk, ordinary chalk that you use for writing on a blackboard. And he said, with all gravity, "This piece of chalk is not a piece of chalk."

Some of the students, who hadn't been paying sufficient attention, fell into a hushed silence. They thought, because they could not understand what had been said, that they were being gifted with some profound truth from the great R. C. Sproul. They squinted their eyes, cocked their heads like confused dogs, and did their best to comprehend the mystery. My father remained silent, letting the gravity of what he had just spoken sink in and allowing those students to sink deeper into their confusion.

He broke his silence by asking, "Do you understand what I just said?"

A few brave souls raised their hands, but my father did not call on them, to save them further embarrassment.

"Of course you don't understand what I just said," he continued. "You can't understand what I just said, not because you are seminary students and I am a seminary professor, but because what I just told you is sheer, unadulterated nonsense. It is not *not* understandable because it is deep, but because it is rubbish. No amount of study, no quantum leap in your IQ, will get you to the point where you can understand it."

And then he laid down the gauntlet: "Not even the omniscient living God can understand what I just said."

He continued. "This is not a limitation on God, however. There are many things God cannot do. He cannot lie. He cannot die. He cannot create an uncreated being. He cannot stop being God. He cannot do any of these things, not because there is some power higher than Himself that restrains Him, but because such would be against Himself, against His nature."

Now he was talking sense.

He explained that it is a false piety to take the glorious truth that God's ways are not our ways, that His mind is past finding out, and turn it into an excuse for affirming contradictions. It is not piety but impiety to ascribe to the living God the creation of confusion. Yes, of course God is beyond us. The finite human mind cannot stretch itself all the way around His infinite mind. It is hubris to think otherwise.

But it would be the absolute destruction of God's own character if He were to affirm both sides of a contradiction. It would in turn be the utter end of our ability to trust Him. If God can have *A* be *A* and not *A* at one and the same time, then, "Believe on the Lord Jesus Christ and you will be saved," could also mean, at one and the same time, "Believe on the Lord Jesus Christ and you will be damned." "This is My Son, in Whom I am well pleased," could also mean, "This is an imposter, the devil himself, and my chief enemy."

"Contradiction," my father explained, "is not only *not* the hallmark of heavenly truth, but it is the sure and certain sign of falsehood. Logic is not the creation of that pagan philosopher Aristotle to lead us away from God; it is part of the very character of God."

He told us that Gordon Clark, our text's author, had gone so far as to argue that the opening of John's Gospel, where we read, "In the beginning was the Word, and the Word was with God, and the Word was God," could just as easily be translated into English, "In the beginning was the Logic, and the Logic was with God, and the Logic was God." The Greek word translated "Word" in our Bible is *logos*, which is likewise the Greek word for "logic." Logic is not the enemy of faith.

"Instead," my father explained, "logic is the truth cop. When it finds a contradiction, he bops it on the head and drags it off to jail."

That fed my soul. I had, for most of my life, felt the weight of the accusation that using logic, when speaking of the things of God, was an attempt to reduce Him down to our level.

Even my own friends have chided me over my zeal for logic. Some of my friends from college once gathered for an event that I did not attend. Afterward I was talking about the get-together with one of my friends who had been there. We were marveling together at those friendships, at how they have not only withstood time and distance but have withstood our own weaknesses. My friend told me that the group had been talking about each of our respective weaknesses.

"What did you all decide was my great weakness?" I asked.

"We all agreed that you were too logical," he said.

With all the flair of Mr. Spock, I replied, "'Too logical' is a contradiction."

I walked out of my father's philosophy class that day three feet off the ground. My guilt had been taken away, not by the suffering of Christ for it, but rather, in this instance, because I realized it had been so misguided. I was not guilty of seeking to drag God down to my level. I was simply trying to understand Him, to know Him better, and that is a good thing.

What I learned that day was that not only did I not have to choose between passion and precision but also that each can and should be a goad to the other—not a vicious cycle, but a virtuous one. I learned that day that dry orthodoxy was not orthodox, and wet heresy was all wet.

I felt as if my father had unclogged the pipe that connected my brain and my heart, that he had shown me how theology leads to doxology, back to theology, and back to doxology. If I am moved by contradiction, I prove myself to be a fool. If, however, I am unmoved by truth, I still prove myself to be a fool.

This was central to my father's gift. Providing snappy answers to those with whom we disagree, whether within or without the church, only feeds our pride. Right understanding should move us to awe. Consider my father's most well-known work, *The Holiness of God*. It was not written in response to some heathen's book, *The Unholiness of God*. Neither was it written as a corrective to some theological school within Christendom that denies divine holiness. Even unbelievers know God is holy and quake (Romans 1)—while believers know God is holy but all too often yawn.

The power of the book was not in that it exposited a difficult-to-understand text or broke down some chain of deductions that led us to a merely sound conclusion. Rather the book went for our jugulars, grabbing us by our collective throats, precisely for the purpose of clearing the passage between our minds and hearts. The response to the book was no calm and dispassionate, "I'm grateful to have this perplexing problem answered." The response was weeping and worship.

For my father, theology was a living thing, because it is the study of the living God. Yes, He is immutable. He is transcendent, high, lofty, and lifted up. But He is both real and near. He has planned all things, and in His plan, He is active and immanent. He is one essence in three persons, which is a deep mystery indeed. But at the very least we know this: He is personal. He knows us, calls us, redeems us, loves us, by name, one at a time. And He welcomes us, invites us, commands us, to draw near to Him, to enter into His presence, to climb into His lap.

Not because we are human. Not because we are made in His image. But because His Son took on flesh and dwelt among us, living a perfect life in our stead and taking on Himself the Father's judgment for our sins. It's all there, in our creeds and confessions, in the Scriptures, and in our systematics. But it's also there when we beat our breasts, crying out, "Lord, be merciful to me, a sinner" (Luke 18:13), and when we sing with joyful tears streaming down our faces,

> "Amazing grace, how sweet the sound
> That saved a wretch like me.
> I once was lost, but now am found,
> T'was blind, but now I see."

18

"As Is"

I had to think carefully through the prayer before I prayed it. I did not want to offend the Almighty. I was in a great situation, and I feared to ask the Lord for an even better situation. I was seeking His favor, but first I had to acknowledge that I already had His favor. Having done so, I moved forward.

I was in seminary at the time. I lived in a nice, safe neighborhood. I had no utility bills to pay. My meals were cooked for me, and, if I didn't care for what was being served, my host would purchase whatever I wanted to cook for myself. There was a swimming pool in the back, my laundry was done for me, I was able to study in quiet—and all of this was rent free.

"Lord, I know You have blessed me tremendously," I prayed. "I am in a situation that anyone would envy. I don't deserve any of what You have given me, much less do I deserve more. But I am asking, with gratitude for what You have given, if I might have more. Would You help me get in a situation where I could move out of my parents' house for good?"

I wasn't trying to escape my parents. I just was past ready to be on my own. It was time.

I didn't look my gift horse in the mouth. Not only did I have no living expenses, but I had this other benefit: Just about every evening,

I enjoyed a free tutorial. I worked a full-time job and took a full-time course load at the seminary, but I was never too tired for those back patio conversations with my dad about my studies. Finally, when he asked, "What did you do in school today?" I had something more useful to say than "Nothin'." It was a nightly debriefing, wherein I would bring back what I had learned to check it with my father.

"Professor So-and-So said this about the Gospel of Matthew, but I thought that has to be off base because . . . ," and my dad would assess my assessment. I still reported to him the arguments I forced into class discussions, and he still sought to impress upon me my calling to see myself as a student rather than as a teacher.

Now, however, he had an even clearer idea of what I could be like in class. Rather than simply hearing my reports of what I did in class, he had to endure what I did in class. That's right. Even my own father had to deal with pesky me trying to pick ideological fights in class. The difference was, he enjoyed them. He enjoyed them, I'm sure, because he always knew he would win.

He described his approach to the classroom as "dia-lecture"—a sort of combination Socratic dialogue wherein he would seek to tease out of us wisdom by asking penetrating questions and then, when that failed, giving us a tiny lecture with the right answers before turning back to discussion.

In those early days, Reformed Theological Seminary in Orlando was housed in an office park, in a rented space not exactly designed for academic pursuits. My father's classroom was the largest on campus since he drew scores of part-time students and laypeople who just wanted to learn from him.

High up in the back of the room, there was a balcony, with tables and chairs pushed up to the edge so you could see down to the professor. I would often lie on the floor of the balcony, neither seeing nor being seen, listening to him as he taught. Well, not so much listening as looking for an opening, waiting for my dad to say something, anything, that I could object to. When he did, I would call out, "Dr. Sproul?" And he would reply, "Yes, Precious?"

Precious is my family name, bequeathed to me by my sister. Not, however, because she found me ever-so-valuable. Rather, it started when we were young. She, despite being the firstborn, was more often in trouble than me (although she *did* eat her stewed tomatoes without complaint). Frustrated that she was so often in trouble while I was so infrequently in trouble, she would complain to my parents, "Of course you think I did it. It couldn't possibly have been Precious. Precious never does anything wrong."

After my dad had called on me, I would challenge what he had said about whatever issue was at hand.

"Did I just hear you say, Dr. Sproul, that unbelievers are . . . ? Does not the Apostle Paul say the opposite in his letter to the Ephesians?"

And off we would go in our debate. As with our arm-wrestling matches, I wasn't looking to win. I just wanted, like Rocky, to go the distance.

I am grateful for the latitude he gave the whole class, including me. Nowhere, however, was that latitude broader than in the class he taught on ethics. There was way more *dia-* in that class than there was *lecture*. His goal, I suspect, was less to get us to reach the right conclusions on this ethical issue or that and more to get our fundamental principles in line so that we would be prepared to apply them broadly in the ministry. He would sometimes set up debates on particular issues between students, or even between teams of students.

One particular class discussion began with a lengthy conversation on truth telling. My father's position was a bit more nuanced than a simple, "Christians must always tell the truth at all times, no matter what." Drawing from the accounts in Exodus of the Hebrew midwives and in Joshua of Rahab the Harlot, he took the position that we owe truth to the one to whom the truth is due. Pharaoh, he argued, was not due the truth from the midwives. The soldiers in Jericho, in like manner, were not due the truth from Rahab.

The trouble with this position, of course, is that it just kicks the ethical can down the road. The principle can't be applied until we answer the broader question: To whom is the truth due?

That led our class into a conversation on truth telling in business deals. Do we, my father asked us all, have a duty to tell a prospective buyer *everything* that is wrong with a used car? My father, perhaps haunted by the memory of the used car he had purchased that had had its odometer spun, argued in the affirmative. I, planting my flag firmly on *caveat emptor* ("let the buyer beware"), argued that while a seller must not lie to a prospective buyer, a seller does not have an ethical duty to disclose everything that could possibly be disclosed.

Like Rocky's first fight with Apollo Creed, this fight did not start well for me. I was buffeted about for the first few rounds and made to look like something of a cheat. Eventually I beat a hasty retreat and set up my defenses here: "What if I were to sell a car," I asked, "while affirming that I, in fact, do not know all that is wrong with it, that I make no warranty about its condition, that I am selling it 'as is'?"

It looked as though my retreat had been strategic indeed. My classmates began to cross over to my side. I was, after all, telling the truth in saying that I was not revealing everything there might be to know. I was explicitly denying the making of any claims. Before a final verdict on the case could be read, however, my father, the man with the microphone, changed the subject. Suddenly we were talking about Nazis at the door asking if we were hiding any Jews.

One of my friends thought it would be more interesting to turn the question on the professor, and to juice it up a bit too, by making *me* the one in hiding.

"Suppose it were your own son, Precious," my friend asked (and of course there were laughs and snickering at this point), "who was wanted by the Nazis. You have hidden him in the basement, and they not only question you about his whereabouts but also leave no room for subtlety. That is, you won't be able to answer in a way that is true, but is meant, nonetheless, to deceive. Would you tell the truth, the whole truth, and nothing but the truth? Would you let them take your own son off to some concentration camp?"

My father took his time in responding. He adopted a thoughtful pose, stroking his chin as he worked his way through the dilemma. Finally, he spoke.

"I would, I believe, let the Nazis know that my son was hidden in the basement," he said. "I would, I think, allow them to take him away. But, I would have one important proviso. There would be one thing the Nazis would have to agree to before I showed them where my son was hiding."

By this time we were all on the edges of our seats. Every gambit we had come up with so far to keep our charge safe from the Nazis and our consciences clean from telling a lie had failed. But now, now the professor was going to tell us how to rightly handle the situation. He was going to bequeath to us the magic words to sail that moral ship between Scylla and Charybdis, between the proverbial rock and a hard place. He paused, making us continue to wait, tantalizing us.

"The only way I'd let them take my son," he said, "was if they'd take him 'as is.'"

Our collective disappointment in not getting the magic answer was swept away in a tsunami of laughter.

Have I mentioned that my father was a charmer?

Part of his charm, interestingly, was its connection to his mind. He had an unusual capacity for not only bringing humor to just about any situation but for doing so on the fly, and in context. Just as he looked at everything around him through a theological lens, so too he looked at most things around him through a lens of humor. This, I would argue, was a function of his own humility.

We all know people who use humor as a weapon, those whose quips are barbed. We find ourselves laughing and wincing at one and the same time. There is an anger, a chip on the shoulder, underlying that kind of humor.

That, however, was not my father's posture. He didn't poke at others, thinking himself better than them. He did not use humor to draw circles to exclude others. Instead he understood his own foibles, his own need for the grace of God, and he realized that he shared that condition with everyone else.

He could laugh at himself because he knew how far he fell short, and yet he also knew that he was beloved of His heavenly Father. When he made a humorous observation on the foibles of others, it was from a posture of sharing those foibles and from a posture of knowing we have peace with our Father.

Such a humor can, and often does, puncture the pride of the haughty, but it is not a sign of pride in itself. He often skewered—although always in love—the self-importance, the inflated self-assessments, to which we are so naturally given. He loved to laugh at our pretensions, while recognizing that we all struggle with pretense.

"As Is"

His humor, in short, was imbued with the gospel. It started with an understanding of how far he himself fell from the mark. It moved next to the glory that, because of Christ, we are received by the Father "as is." It moved finally to our common struggle to become what we are declared to be already—righteous. He understood well that we are beloved of the Father right now, but that we are not loved just as we are—but just as He, the Son, is. It is the righteousness of Christ by which we stand. And that is cause for joy, for peace, for celebration, and for laughter.

19

Now Is the Time

When I first began to read my father's books, I confess that I wasn't in search of a deeper knowledge of the things of God. Instead I read them for the stories—and, more specifically, for those stories in which I played a part. There was something about having my name, or even just an account involving me, in print. It made me feel good, even if the story wasn't a flattering one. As time progressed and as I began to mature, however, I found I was learning things that I was delighted to be learning.

Despite never having read a book on writing or public speaking—or, perhaps, because of this—my father managed to avoid being formulaic. There are books out there on how to write Christian nonfiction that will tell you to start with a story as an illustration (preferably something personal), to include something from the Bible by the time you get to page two, and after that, to make your point quickly.

When reading books, I can usually determine which writers have read these kinds of how-to guides. They tend to sound very much the same. My father, however, seldom followed such formulas. Although he was a man who tended to listen to the experts, there were realms where he had the wisdom to march to the beat of his own drummer, and writing was one of those.

When discussions first began over the creation of the *Renewing Your Mind* radio program, we were smart enough to hire a few consultants to give us some hints on how to succeed in radio. One of them said it was important for my father to teach from a standing position, because doing so creates forty-five percent more energy than when you sit. (I wanted to ask him, "Did you know that seventy-eight percent of all statistics are made up on the spot?")

Another expert disagreed. He insisted that radio is not really a teaching medium but rather a storytelling medium. Given that my father's strength was teaching, my father was warned to adapt or perish. "You can't really teach on the radio," he was told.

My father determined to demonstrate that all the experts were wrong. And they were. It may well be that most can't teach on the radio, but my father could. And he did.

The stories my father told in his books did not come out of a formula, but out of his life. I was used to that. Those glimpses into his life, however, were muted, covered by a thin veil. My father was not one given to the Red Smith school of writing. Smith, a revered sports writer, was quoted in 1949 as saying that writing was easy. "You simply sit down at the typewriter, open your veins, and bleed," he said. Instead my father was honest—but cautious.

That all changed, however, with *Surprised by Suffering*. That book began by taking readers immediately into the heart of a real crisis. My father recounted, openly, the agony and heartache he went through when my sister, his daughter, discovered that her unborn daughter had passed to glory while still in the womb. It was an account that could bring a strong man to tears, as my father explored the pain of not just my sister's helplessness in caring for her baby, but of his own helplessness in caring for *his* baby, my sister. Tragedy is always tragic, but it is a deeper burden still for those whose calling it is to care for and protect those left without the means to do so.

Although I'm sure it wasn't a calculated move, that story set the stage for the rest of that book, in which my father argued vigorously that God is in control of all our suffering, that indeed suffering is a vocation, something that God calls us to.

Some, I suspect, would begin reading that book skeptical that my father knew of what he spoke. He was incredibly successful in his calling after all. His wife and children loved him. His faith was vibrant and living. So what could he possibly know of suffering? That opening account of his granddaughter's death, however, reminded readers that suffering—like the One who is sovereign over it—is no respecter of persons.

It is within the context of suffering that the proverbial rubber of our perspective on God's sovereignty meets the road of our real lives and of our real needs. When we debate free will—when we speculate over whether God merely knows in advance who will choose Him, or whether He chooses who will choose Him—it is easy to be detached, emotionally uninvolved. When we are in the crucible of deep hardship, however, it suddenly becomes all too real.

When I was in my thirties, one might have thought that I too knew little of real suffering. I was busy with the work God had given me, growing a ministry, planting a church, raising a family. I had a rambling home on seven acres of wooded land in the mountains of southwest Virginia. I had a wife, two little children—a boy and a girl—and a loving blue heeler dog named Socks. God poured out still more blessing when our third child was born, a little girl, Shannon.

Though she scored well on her Apgar, Shannon soon began to lag behind her peers in hitting maturation landmarks. We followed the counsel of our doctor, tried to fatten her up, but by the time she was one, we took her four hours away to a children's hospital to have her diagnosed. The MRI she was given showed the problem right away. She was diagnosed with lissencephaly. The ridges we see on a healthy brain were not there. Half of all lissencephalic children die before they turn seven. Of the half who survive, half die in the next seven years.

I didn't follow doctors' orders but stayed up into the wee hours that first night, scouring the Internet to learn all I could about the condition. It was not encouraging. Shannon, it seemed, would never learn to walk. (Although she eventually did.) She would never learn to talk or feed herself, never be potty-trained. I would never walk her down an aisle to give her away to her husband.

The next morning it was my duty to pass along the hard news to family and friends, beginning with my parents. I got them both on the phone and began to give my report. I explained all I had learned thus far. I was able to get through the explanation without crying because I had already run out of tears.

I was torn though. I wanted to run to them for comfort. I wanted my dad to fix it, just as I'm sure my sister wanted our dad to fix it with her little girl. On the other hand, as a father, dealing with my own sense of impotence in this situation, I didn't want to add that burden to him. I didn't want him to think that, just because he was my daddy who had always fixed my broken toys, I was now looking to him to fix my broken little girl.

The first thing he did was to ask how our family was handling all this. He could not heal my daughter, but he could seek to minister to our spirits.

"Dad," I responded, "I am not just *a* Calvinist, but I am the son of *the* Calvinist. I have spent my life sitting at your feet, listening to you speak on God's absolute sovereignty. I have listened to you speak, in turn, on His absolute trustworthiness. I have been taught well by you that because of the work of Christ, my heavenly Father loves me perfectly. I have believed in all these things myself, argued in defense of them. If there is anyone on this planet who should be prepared for this, it is me. I've been listening and paying attention."

That's when he made explicit what had always been implicit in all he had taught me. He did not provide some new insight. He didn't direct me to twist my situation just a smidge so I could look at it from a different angle and discover facets I had missed. Instead he simply said, "Now is the time for you to believe what you have always believed."

It was a short sentence, but it was a rich one. It took me back to the book of Proverbs, to Solomon's repeated insistence that his son heed his father, that he treasure the words he was being given. It reminded me of what my father had always enjoined me and others—to not allow our spiritual standing to rise and fall with our circumstances.

His words were both an encouragement and an admonition. He was encouraging me to rest and be at peace, knowing that even this was part and parcel of my heavenly Father's good and perfect plan. And he was admonishing me not to merely give lip service to God's sovereignty but to believe it from the top of my head down to the tips of my toes.

My father never saw theology as a toy, as a parlor game for the mind. Rather, it was the truth that was to shape who we are, to inform what we do, to drive what we feel. It was real to him, and he was reminding me, in that moment, that it needed to be real to me.

He helped remind me that there was no such thing as purposeless evil or suffering, that we find our courage in the Triune God who makes glad our soul by teaching us that it is God who works all things together for our good. As acutely painful as it is to endure the sufferings and hardships ordained by God, one day we will truly, finally, and forever understand the depths of the riches of the wisdom and knowledge of God.

Over the course of Shannon's fifteen-year sojourn on this planet, I had the opportunity to witness my own father believing what he had always believed. He knew that Shannon was made in the image of God, that she, like every child, was a blessing and not a burden. He knew that she was beloved of her heavenly Father. He knew that she was His instrument in my sanctification. He knew that her joy, her trust, her passion were as intense, if not more so, than his own.

And I got to believe what I have always believed. I learned daily how my heavenly Father cares for me. I learned daily that what we are tempted to see as hard providences are really blessings, for which we must not only give thanks but for which we cannot help but give thanks.

That evening I went back to something else I had heard my father say. He had once asked an audience, of which I was blessed to be a part, "What would you do, how would your life change, if Jesus Christ Himself were to stand before you, take your face in His scarred hands, look you straight in the eye, and promise you, 'I will never leave you or forsake you?' What would you say if He said, 'Everything I send into your life, which will be everything in your life, will in the end redound to the everlasting glory of My Father; and it will likewise work toward your everlasting good?' Can you imagine having Jesus Himself speak those words to you?"

In the midst of our reverie, while everyone in the audience was imagining that poignant picture, my father reminded us, "Jesus *has* said exactly those words to you. He said them in Hebrews 13:5 and in Romans 8:28. They may not be written in red letters, but these words in the Word come ultimately from Jesus, the Word made flesh."

I remembered those promises again when Jesus called my little girl home to Him. I remembered those promises again when Jesus called my daddy home to Him. Those days, like every day, are the days when I am called to believe what I have always believed: Our God reigns.

He loves us with an everlasting, immeasurable love. And He has promised to give us the greatest gift, beyond our imagination—He remakes us into the image of His Son, the express image of His glory.

20

Honor Your Father

There was one book of my father's that I passed over as I was growing up. I was ten years old when a box full of dirt-brown books arrived at the house. The book had my father's name at the bottom of it. Above that—and this might help you understand why I took a pass on it—was written *Soli Deo Gloria: Essays in Reformed Theology: Festschrift for John H. Gerstner.*

My grasp of Latin and of the history of the Reformation were, at that point, insufficient to help me understand what *soli Deo gloria* meant. Today I know that it means, "To God alone the glory." In fact it was one of the five *solas* of the Protestant Reformation, brief slogans that summarized the Reformers' core convictions. Even if I had known that at the time, however, I suspect that the foreign word *festschrift* would have been sufficient to scare me off.

What in the world is a *festschrift* anyway?

There is an old tradition among academics that when a man reaches retirement or some other milestone in his career, his peers write papers on a subject dear to his heart and publish those papers as a book. That is a *festschrift*. It is a kind of gold watch for the academic set.

Even if I had known what a *festschrift* was, I probably still would have steered clear—unless I had been looking for treatment for insomnia. Anyways, my father had been given the responsibility to edit this particular book in honor of John Gerstner, mentor to my father and to many others.

Years later, by the time I was approaching my forties, I not only had read and benefited from that book but also had determined to follow in my father's footsteps, putting together a *festschrift* for him, but with a few twists.

First, because my father was so passionate about teaching the laity—although he was certainly comfortable in the realm of the academy—the book would not be academic. It would be geared toward the general layman, the same audience for whom he typically wrote.

Second, and in line with that first goal, the contributors would include not just my father's peers but also his former students, those whom he had mentored along the way.

Third, rather than simply laying out a broad theme and giving the contributors free reign to choose their topics, I assigned each of them to write on one of the five points of Calvinism, as well as one of the five *solas* of the Reformation. I determined the book would be bookended by two contributions from me—an opening introductory biographical chapter and a concluding exposition of *soli Deo gloria*.

I gathered the team of contributors and secured a publisher—the very publisher that had not only published the Gerstner *festschrift* but had also published my father's first book, the thirty-year anniversary of which we chose as our landmark to celebrate. All of this, of course, was done in secret. I wasn't able to make use of his editorial eye in the process of putting the book together, nor could I pick his theological brain. The surprise was scheduled to be unveiled at our annual national conference in Orlando.

Several of the contributors were already scheduled to speak at the event. Several more were brought down to be part of the unveiling. My father was scheduled to speak the first night of the conference, and, as was often the case, I was tapped to give his introduction. (As an aside, my favorite introduction I ever gave him ended this way: "This is my father, in whom I am well pleased. Hear him.")

Instead of introducing my father, however, I invited all the contributors to come up onto the platform. And then I addressed the crowd, as my father sat in the front row listening. I explained our purpose that evening and why the men on the platform were there with me. I gave a brief biography of my father's life, highlighting how things had changed since I was a little boy sneaking through a lecture to get a bowl of cereal from the kitchen.

I told the assembled that we were marking the thirtieth anniversary of my father's first book, then titled *The Symbol*, an exposition of the Apostles' Creed. I spoke of the breadth of my father's influence, his working together with other great men in defense of the inerrancy of Scripture and of justification by faith alone. I talked of the many congregants who were being fed by undershepherds who had studied under my father in seminary.

As I began to choke up, I mentioned my sadness that there were two men missing from the list of contributors. How fitting it would have been had John Gerstner lived long enough to write a chapter for his mentee, just as his mentee had written for Gerstner.

Also missing was a contribution from James Montgomery Boice, who had passed away as a relatively young man a few years prior. Cancer, I noted, had been the cause of his untimely death. Dr. Boice was little more than half-a-year older than my father and had had a prodigious reach as pastor of the historic Tenth Presbyterian Church in Philadelphia and as teacher on the widely broadcast *The Bible Study Hour* radio program. He was also a great friend to my father, the two of them relishing all that they had in common and all that separated them—Dr. Boice being a bit more formal and my father more familiar.

I finished my address then invited my father up to receive his book. He too had tears in his eyes but dried them quickly. As I stood beside him at that podium, he thanked all the contributors. He expressed how honored he was to receive this book and how he hoped God would use it to bring still more reformation to His church. Then he turned his attention to me.

"I am grateful to my son for spearheading this project. He has, not just on this day but all his life, sought to honor me and his mother, grasping the import of the Fourth Commandment. That said, I'm hoping he will make a more careful study of the Reformed faith. For, if my ears did not deceive me, I believe, just a few minutes ago, he made reference to James Boice's 'untimely death.' Where, I can't help but wonder, could my son have ever learned that a man could ever die in an 'untimely' way? Does he not know that God numbers our days, and that nothing could ever change His decree from before all time?"

He was, needless to say, smiling the whole time he was scolding me for my ill-chosen words. As I discussed earlier, his humor was never cutting, even when one was the butt of the joke. I blushed and chalked it up to his penchant for brushing aside poignant public moments, keeping that veil between him and his audience. That did not, however, keep me from honoring him further still by showing him that I was a committed student of the master.

As he stepped back to thundering applause, I returned to the microphone. When it grew quiet again, I directed the contributors to go ahead and take their seats. I then proceeded to thank my father for his response. I thanked him for so gently correcting my theological faux pas in speaking of an untimely death. I noted that such things can be pretty embarrassing when they happen in front of several thousand people.

"Thank you also, sir, for your kind words regarding my zeal to honor you and your wife, my mother," I said. "I know I have often fallen well short of the ideal. But I know also that it has always been my deep desire to honor you. Which is why I have decided not to make mention of the fact that God's command for children to honor their parents is not actually the fourth commandment, but the fifth."

It was a great moment, a delightful mixture of genuine public honoring and good-natured humor. But it did, poignantly, reveal my father's reluctance to reveal too much. That deflection—away from himself, away from the genuine appreciation expressed by his peers, by his students, by his audience—was driven, I suspect, by both a real humility and by a real desire for some form of privacy.

There is a burden in being so deeply appreciated by so many. First, you know you are not nearly as good a man as your admirers think you are. And second, you suspect you may be as bad as your harshest critics insist. I remember my father saying that, when we receive a hundred bits of encouragement and one bit of rejection, we all tend to focus on the rejection and struggle to accept the encouragement.

Rejection—even just one bit—automatically destroys the hundred bits of encouragement you might otherwise receive. You begin to think that the accolades you're receiving are really just earned by your persona rather than by your person. As a result, you look for affirmation from the people who really know you—those who can praise your person and not just your persona—which, in my father's case, was his family and a very small circle of friends.

Although I feasted on them just like everyone else, I did not wildly praise my father's every book, article, or lecture. That, I suspect, was another burden he had to carry. It's not that I didn't praise and encourage him; rather, all the words of encouragement he received had to, of necessity, suffer from inflation at my lack of effervescent praise. His gift was such that we all grew accustomed to it. His skills set the bar so high that we lost our ability to be amazed when he topped himself. It was just what he did. That he did it so well became merely normal.

From the other side, he faced this problem: He didn't want people thinking about the messenger, but rather about the message. He didn't seek out accolades; he had a heart like that of John the Baptist. He wanted to decrease so that Jesus would increase. And perhaps this is how we developed our own peculiar liturgy, in which I was blessed to encourage him. On those occasions when he would speak at a conference during which I wasn't called to introduce him, I would sit beside him in the front row. We would both listen as whoever introduced him would pile on the accolades, listing his accomplishments. And just as it was time for my father to stand and ascend to the pulpit, I would whisper into his ear these three words: "Tell the truth."

It wasn't, of course, that I was fearful he was preparing to stand up and spew out lies. It wasn't that I thought he would be fearful of offending and would thus soften the hard truths he was called to speak. Rather, I wanted to remind him of what he already knew—where the power was, and what the goal was. It may well be that some of those gathered wanted to watch him do what he did so well, like fans at a football game. But what they needed to hear was the truth of the gospel. And that was where the real power was.

Which is also why I told him, "Dad, I love all that you teach, not because it is you teaching it, but because it is faithful to the Reformed faith. And I love the Reformed faith because it is faithful to the Word of God."

It wasn't that I was trying to distance myself from him. I knew his character well enough to know, in fact, that this would encourage him. I knew he would want it no other way. I was, and am, committed to him because we were, and are, committed to the Word of God, the Bible, and to the living Word of God, Jesus Christ.

21

He Is My Friend

I have noted already that when you are well known, even if the pond in which you swim is as small as the Reformed world, there is an accompanying challenge in your relationships. Sometimes I wonder if the people who seek to be my friend actually want to be my friend or if what they want is to collect me—to claim me as a prize, as a name they can drop in conversation with their real friends. While carrying with him a certain reticence, I do not doubt my father felt that challenge. I know that although I am not *the* R. C. Sproul, merely *an* R. C. Sproul, it has been a deep challenge for me. How much more it must have been a challenge for my father.

I know, as well, that one common strategy to combat this sense that people don't like you for who you are, but for your position, is to make friends with those who are not in a position to be much helped by you. There is a reason why famous people hang out together, or even marry each other. When Ben Affleck and Matt Damon hang out, neither has to fear that the other has an angle, that they are being used. That may help explain why some of my father's closest friends were the men he worked with, other influential thinkers and theologians.

Don't get me wrong. Sharing a platform with someone doesn't necessarily foster lasting relationships. Fighting in the trenches together and standing on the same convictions, however, can forge genuine friendships. My father was truly delighted to spend time with James Montgomery Boice. Additionally, he not only carried a deep respect for John MacArthur but also enjoyed him personally. Anyone who ever saw the debate between MacArthur and my father on the topic of infant baptism can readily see how two Christians, on opposing sides of an important theological issue, can disagree amicably, all the while remaining close friends and allies in proclaiming the good news.

One of his earliest comrades in arms, however, was Chuck Colson. Mr. Colson professed faith in Christ the year before he was sent to federal prison on an obstruction of justice charge related to his involvement in the Watergate scandal during the Nixon administration. He had been described as President Richard Nixon's "hatchet man." After his release he devoted his life to prison ministry, founding Prison Fellowship.

In God's providence he came upon my father's audio series on the holiness of God and was deeply moved. He reached out to my father and, over the years, looked to him as a theological mentor. Mr. Colson would visit the Ligonier Valley Study Center from time to time and would even sometimes take over my bedroom while I was exiled to my father's study floor in a sleeping bag.

The two developed a close working relationship, with prisoners regularly coming to the study center for training before returning to prison to teach others. There was even, for a time, some talk of the two ministries merging. There are many nuggets of wisdom I still cherish from their relationship together. None, however, was as powerful to me as the story my father related about a speaking engagement Mr. Colson had.

It matters little where he was speaking. The relevant part was that Mr. Colson was identified with Richard Nixon and that Richard Nixon was nearly universally vilified. The audience proved to be a hostile one, funneling their anti–Vietnam War, anti-Nixon rage toward Mr. Colson as he sought to speak to them about the work of Christ. At one point a member of the audience interrupted his speech, shouting out this question: "Why would you go to jail for a man like Richard Nixon?"

Mr. Colson paused and looked down at his podium while a hush fell, the crowd waiting for the fireworks to start. Finally he replied, "Because Richard Nixon is my friend." The assembled, the story goes, broke into a spontaneous standing ovation. All the hostility, all the unmasked political rage, was broken by a simple, yet profound, affirmation of the power and beauty of loyal friendship. Right wing, left wing, peacenik, hawk—everyone appreciates the value of loyal friends.

It is not a mistake that the Bible refers to the first person of the Trinity as "the Father." While all earthly fathers have feet of clay, and some violently distort the beauty of this image, the truth is that the virtues of fatherhood are essential to God's "God-ness." First among those virtues is a term that crops up time and again throughout the Old Testament concerning the Father. He, it is said, is the essence of *hesed*, the Hebrew word perhaps best translated as "loyal love." The "love" in "loyal love" communicates the reality of God's emotional response to His children. It is true that God is above us, transcendent, different from us—but His love for us is genuine, real, even emotional.

We Christians are more than happy to affirm that God forgives us because of the work of Christ. That is the very core of our faith, how we are redeemed. Often, however, we too easily gloss over two glorious truths.

First, He loved us before the work of Christ. Remember that the Bible tells us, "While we were still sinners, Christ died for us" (Romans 5:8). Remember that it is because He so loved us that He sent His only begotten Son (John 3:16). His love did not begin at the atonement. Rather, the atonement sprang from His love.

Second, His love for us is loyal. It does not waver. When the serpent accuses us, our Father turns a deaf ear. When the Son intercedes for us, He listens. The love of the Father for His children is as immutable as the Father Himself. Nothing will undermine His love, redirect it, diminish it, overpower it. It is reckless, prodigal, and loyal.

When I think of my earthly father, I easily see how he reflected these traits of our heavenly Father. Like his friend Chuck Colson, my father was a profoundly loyal man, and he sought to instill the same in me. He had a phrase he liked to use, an aphorism that he would drop as a friendly reminder: "We, son, stick with the stuck."

Success has more friends than it could possibly use. Failure, however, is the loneliest place of all. When our world is looking up, we find our coattails crowded (forgive the mixed metaphor) with bandwagon riders. Jesus Himself experienced this. When the miracles were flowing, when the bread was being multiplied, the crowds thronged around Him. When He was arrested, however, even His most "loyal" friends deserted him. Peter—he of the zealous commitment to follow Christ even unto death—denied Jesus three times that night, even after having been forewarned.

The mark of real friends is not their willingness to climb the mountains with us but their actually walking with us through the valleys. You stick with the stuck. And that was just the kind of man my father always was. While Mr. Colson received the praise of men at that moment in his speech, sticking with the stuck is, more often than not, relational suicide. When we align ourselves with the broken, the hurting, the scandalous, we bring on ourselves brokenness, pain, and scandal.

It takes a certain amount of courage, of security, of peace, to be able to stick with the stuck. And that can only flow out of one place: the realization that we are all the stuck. When we are tempted to turn our backs on those whose failures bring embarrassment on us, we are called to remember the One who hung for our failures, the One who so identified with us that He took on Himself the full fury of the Father that we deserved. While Peter was denying Jesus, saying, "I never knew him," Jesus was affirming Peter to His Father, saying, "I've known him from before all time. He is mine."

Over the years I have brought shame on my father on more than one occasion. I am, in the minds of many, living proof that sometimes the apple falls plenty far from the tree. That I have brought shame, however, does not mean that he ever saw me as a shame. While my father was always loyal, he wasn't the most open man, nor has our family been the most open family. We thrive in the current of unspoken affirmations. I'm learning, however, to be more open.

I had just said goodbye to my parents prior to moving out of state. As I climbed into the car with my beloved new wife, I told her that I hated the thought that I had disappointed my parents, that I had brought them shame.

"You need to go back in and tell them that," she said.

I explained that she didn't yet understand the dynamics of my family. She didn't care. Again she told me I needed to go back in the house and tell them. Finally I relented.

"I had to come back in here because there's something else I need to tell you," I said to my parents. "I'm so sorry for letting you down.

I know that you were counting on me, and now I've brought you shame. I just want you both to know that it kills me to know that. All I've ever wanted to do was to make you proud."

"Oh, son," my parents said, "we are not in the least ashamed of you. We love you, and nothing will ever change that. Do not feel that fear, nor bear that burden. Be at peace."

Had I continued to refuse the insistence of my beloved wife to speak to my parents, I never would have known, to the extent that I did in that moment, my parents' true feelings about my situation. I would have continued to carry a great weight and burden upon my back stemming from my actions. But because I listened to the counsel of a godly helpmeet, my burden was lifted, my fears were abated, my heart was at peace.

Some of you may think you know the rest of the story as it relates to my father and Chuck Colson. In 1994, Colson, working with Richard John Neuhaus, published a controversial document, *Evangelicals and Catholics Together*. This document affirmed that Rome and Protestants share a common commitment to the gospel of Jesus Christ. Its aim was to not just foster unity but to demonstrate it.

The result was that it revealed a deep chasm in the evangelical world, between those who saw the Reformation as necessary and definitive and those who saw it as a tempest in a teapot. My father and Chuck Colson were on opposite sides of that chasm. Their working relationship drew to a close in the fallout.

It could be argued that this relational end demonstrated a failure of *hesed*, of loyal love—that while Mr. Colson was willing to be loyal to President Nixon, he was not willing to be loyal to my father, or that my father, while willing to be loyal to me, was not willing to be loyal to Mr. Colson. And such an argument would be deeply flawed.

He Is My Friend

I cannot say where Mr. Colson's heart was, but I do know where my father's heart was.

First, he remained loyal to Mr. Colson until the end. The disagreement was real, deep, and on an issue of vital importance. And my father's loyalty to his friend kept him from affirming or embracing his friend's error. Instead, he sought to correct it, reaching out to Mr. Colson, explaining the theology of the Reformation, pleading with him to turn from his error. Mr. Colson's error did not move him from friend to enemy in my father's book. Rather, the error was the enemy, and loyalty to his friend required fighting against the enemy that held his friend captive.

Second, my father understood that the ultimate object of our *hesed* is the One who has *hesed* for us, Jesus, and His gospel. My father remained steadfast and immovable and even redoubled his efforts to proclaim, explain, and defend the Good News. That is the one thing that the stuck—whatever they are stuck with, or stuck in, or have been stuck by—need always. It's what I needed as well. My father is not ashamed of me, because my elder Brother is not ashamed of me. Jesus is always loyal to His bride and loves her faithfully forever.

22

Great

I recently had lunch with two new friends. It was the first time we had met, and they were not at all shy about asking what my life had been like growing up. I gave them my standard two-part response. First, the great thing about having R. C. Sproul for a father was not that he was such an amazing theologian but that he was such an amazing dad. Second, having only had one father all my life, I had nothing to which I could compare my experience. It was just normal for me and my sister.

That's a good thing, but it's also a bad thing. It's a good thing because the blessings that came with being my father's son were, for the most part, natural and organic. I did not feel like I was growing up in a fishbowl or that I was scrutinized more closely than anyone else. The bad part was that it gave me an idea of what "normal" was that I knew I could never attain.

Just as I preferred soccer to all other sports when I was young because that was one sport my father had never played, so too my early career goals steered rather afar from becoming a theologian. My first answer to the question, "What do you want to be when you grow up?" wasn't anything silly or unrealistic like astronaut or cowboy. No, I knew what I wanted. I wanted to be a pirate.

While I would have been content to play for my beloved Pittsburgh Pirates, that's not what I meant. I wanted to sail the seven seas in search of plunder. Other kids played cops and robbers, cowboys and Indians. My friends and I played pirates. My older sister was even kind enough once to draw a treasure map for a friend and me, which we followed to the X, where we gleefully dug up a bag full of candy.

That goal changed, however, when something on the television caught my eye. I fell in love with a bear named Ben, and suddenly I aspired not to a life of crime but to life as a mountain man. Now I wanted to be Grizzly Adams. The show began airing when I was already eleven years old. I wasn't the most sophisticated kid and found nothing incongruous about my dream.

It took a few years for me to realize that my goal, like that of being a pirate, was a touch on the unrealistic side. But I didn't budge much. I simply came up with the closest "real job" to being a mountain man. And so I decided to be a lumberjack.

Like my father, the first thing I did when embracing something new was to gather all the accouterments. I got a red and black checked flannel shirt. I acquired a pair of suspenders. And, over the course of several birthdays and Christmases, I begged and pleaded with my parents for an axe. Eventually they relented.

It took the lure of the open road to make my next future career move. As I mentioned before, when I got my driver's license, I discovered I loved to drive. And I loved listening to music. I figured I could do both, and make a living, as a truck driver. Eventually I realized that having some mechanical skills would be useful in that line of work, and unfortunately I had none.

Great

By the time I had become a Christian, I had come to realize there were more important things than simply making a living. That led me through a series of dream jobs, starting with becoming a sports star. I incorporated my hopes into my prayers, reasoning with the Almighty, "If you make me into an all-pro for the Steelers, Lord, just think of all the good I could do for the kingdom. When we win the Super Bowl, and the whole world is watching, I could give You all the glory."

Just as my lack of mechanical skills had eliminated truck driver as a career, so too the hard reality that I had precious few athletic skills put that dream to bed quite early. So I prayed this way: "Lord, if You could make me a rock star, I could write lyrics that subtly push back against the darkness, that do the work of pre-evangelism."

You guessed it—I have no musical skills.

So I moved on. "Lord, if you help me to write the great American novel, I could weave things in that would help people contemplate their need for You."

By this time I was beginning to notice a pattern: I was telling the God of heaven and earth that I was perfectly willing to be adored by millions, to rake in the big bucks, for His sake and for the sake of His kingdom.

Pretty big of me, wouldn't you say?

My father was none of those things. He was a teacher, a speaker, a writer. His field was theology. And because he was my only father, my picture of what success looked like looked an awful lot like him. As I began to dip my toes into various ministry outlets—as a magazine editor, as a writer of books, as a speaker, as a pastor—I could not help but measure myself against him.

Though some might say otherwise, I'm not crazy. There is a sane part of my mind that realizes that comparing myself to my father is not realistic. Two of Michael Jordan's sons played NCAA Division I basketball. That requires no small amount of talent.

But no one could expect them to be as great as their father had been. There is only one Michael Jordan. In like manner, I knew it was utterly unrealistic to hope that I would have the giftings, the wisdom, and the reach that my father enjoyed.

That sane part of my mind, however, did not keep me from the pain of seeing myself fall so short, so often. Writing books that hundreds of thousands of people read and are blessed by—that's what a man does. Reaching millions on a national radio broadcast—that's what a man does. Preaching to thousands—that's what a man does.

The struggle wasn't simply failing to reach my goals; the struggle was unlearning to measure myself as a man against my father.

Where, though, could I find the wisdom to deal with this struggle? Who could help me tame my less sane part and get it in line with my more sane part?

I took my problem to my dad. I gently presented to him the weight of my frustration. I began by wondering why the books I wrote sold so few copies. (I always warn aspiring writers: Writing the book is the easiest part. Getting a publisher is the hard part. Getting it into the hands of consumers is the harder part. Getting consumers to actually read what you've written, that's the hardest part.)

With his usual tact and grace, my father said, "You think having my name gives you an advantage. But maybe it doesn't. Why would anyone buy one of your books when they could buy one of mine?"

Yeah, sometimes the truth hurts.

He went on to help me, however, by saying this: "There is nothing in the world wrong with wanting to do great things for the kingdom of God."

Great

First, my dad had skewered my pride. But now he eased my conscience. I went away from that conversation realizing the issue I had to contend with was less my professional standing and more the leanings of my heart. I realized that wanting to do great things for the kingdom and wanting to be great in the kingdom looked an awful lot alike—but, in reality, are polar opposites.

Paul taught much the same lesson when he wrestled with the thorn in his flesh. He wrote to the church at Corinth:

> Concerning this thing I pleaded with the Lord three times that it might depart from me. And He said to me, "My grace is sufficient for you, for My strength is made perfect in weakness." Therefore most gladly I will rather boast in my infirmities, that the power of Christ may rest upon me. Therefore I take pleasure in infirmities, in reproaches, in needs, in persecutions, in distresses, for Christ's sake. For when I am weak, then I am strong (2 Corinthians 12:8–10).

The path to making an impact for the kingdom of God is found not in success but in failure, not in strength but in weakness. Because it is when we are abased that He abounds.

Over the years I have sought to leave this legacy to the church. I want every believer to come to embrace what I call "The R. C. Sproul Jr. Principle of Hermeneutics." This principle notes that we have a tendency to see the folly of men and women in the Bible as something we have grown past. We all think we would have been like Joshua and Caleb, trusting in the Lord on their return from the Promised Land, not filled with fear like the other ten. When we think this way, we flatter ourselves. The Bible is a mirror, showing us ourselves.

The principle goes like this: Whenever you see anyone doing something really foolish in the Bible, do not say to yourself, "How can he be so foolish?" Ask instead, "How am I foolish just as he is?"

The Corinthian church lifted up the men with the best reputations, with the greatest eloquence. Paul had neither. All he had was an acute awareness of his own weaknesses and an unwavering confidence in the power of his Redeemer.

God used the drunken Noah, the lying Abraham, the scheming Jacob, the bragging Joseph, the stuttering Moses, the cowering Gideon, the sensuous Samson, the murdering and adulterous David, the defiant Jonah, the impetuous and denying Peter to show forth His power, His grace—to build His unshakable kingdom.

We serve a God who makes straight lines out of crooked sticks. What He will not do, however, is allow crooked sticks to pridefully declare how straight they are.

My father was never an ambitious man. He never plotted and planned his way into a position of influence and respect. He regularly took hard stands on the very issues that caused the powerful to mock and deride him. His goal was to be faithful in affirming that Jesus alone is the Faithful One and that the rest of us desperately need His life, His death, and His resurrection. He embodied the wisdom that is the mirror image of the folly G. K. Chesterton described in *Orthodoxy*:

> What we suffer from today is humility in the wrong place. Modesty has moved from the organ of ambition. Modesty has settled upon the organ of conviction; where it was never meant to be. A man was meant to be doubtful about himself, but undoubting about the truth; this has been exactly reversed.[7]

My father was modest in his ambitions, resolute in his convictions. And that is why God was pleased to use him. My prayer is not that God would allow me to replicate my father's influence but that He would allow me, in some small way, to reflect his character. The great thing I want to do in the kingdom of God is to acknowledge that I am anything but great, that my only hope is my great Redeemer.

God's great promise is that, in Him—just as He has said to my father—my heavenly Father is able to me, "Well done, thou good and faithful servant." My prayer is that I will give thanks that He has called me to be a doorkeeper in His house rather than to dwell in the tents of the wicked (Psalm 84:10).

23

Two Words

I've often said that if the Internet ever created a quiz, "Who are you in the Hundred Acre Wood?" I would have no need to take it. I already know who I am: Eeyore. I'm a pessimist by nature—not so much a glass-half-empty guy but more a glass-probably-has-poison-in-it guy. Entering C. S. Lewis's Narnian literary universe, I've always identified with Puddleglum the Marshwiggle.

Perhaps a defining quality that distinguishes the optimist from the pessimist is that the former sees change as opportunity while the latter sees it as challenge. The optimist expects change to translate into improvement while the pessimist expects change to translate into regression. From another angle: The optimist sees where he is as a launching point while the pessimist sees his location as a bunker, a place of safety to be clung to.

One realm where my pessimism tends to rear its gloomy head is when someone asks to meet with me face-to-face. When a pessimist gets a phone call, a text, an email asking for a time to meet, he immediately wants to know what the meeting is about. He wants to be prepared, so as not to be blindsided. For those of us in the gloomy crowd, fear creeps in if the reason for the meeting remains shrouded in mystery.

My parents, despite their terribly busy schedules, always made accessibility to them a priority for my sister and me. They had an open door policy for us, twenty-four seven. Apart from Christ, and each other, we were their highest priorities.

Despite their not suffering from congenital pessimism, they must have known, from experience, that if I called and asked specifically for a face-to-face meeting with both of them, it probably wasn't good news. I've met with them to confess sins. I've met with them to confess failures. And I've met with them to express—with care and respect—grievances. So I suspect they worried a bit that spring afternoon in 2016 when I asked if I might stop by their house to talk with them face-to-face.

I was nervous about the meeting too. I knew that what I had to say was good news, not bad news, but on the scale of surprise, it would be off the charts. How would they react? I needed their counsel, but I also wanted that counsel to go a certain way. I was moving in a particular direction, and I wanted their encouragement. I sat down with them and got right to it.

"You know that lady I've been trying to help with her life challenges on the internet the past three years?" I said. "The one who came to me seeking objective advice as she was managing her husband's desertion, infidelity, their divorce, and his crime?"

They acknowledged that they remembered my having spoken of this woman in the past.

Then I broke the news: "Well, I'm grooving on her. Really, really grooving on her."

I looked up with expectation, only to see their countenances light up like Christmas trees.

Two Words

"Tell us about her," they said.

"I'm not sure you have enough time for me to tell you all the things that I find so captivating about her. But here are a few of the things that draw me to her. First, she has been so faithful in the midst of such hardship. She has never complained to God but leans on Him constantly. She feels His presence so powerfully and has the utmost confidence in Him. She is a woman of prayer. She is a woman of the Word. And she has brought both to bear in my own life. She prays for me. She speaks life into me, right out of the Bible. I'll tell you, though, one of the first things I noticed about her, from the very beginning: She has the gift of encouragement. I told her a few years ago, 'Whatever man you get behind will be able to conquer the world.' She is chock-full of wisdom, and it just flows right out of her. I can't tell you how many times I've struggled with this thing or that, and she knew just what to say, how to direct my gaze back to Jesus, how to help me own my responsibilities."

Now you might be thinking at this point that what I gave my parents was the spiritual equivalent of that damning-with-faint-praise comment when describing a blind date, "She has a great personality." But I continued on. "And she is incredibly beautiful."

I took out my phone to show them a picture, my favorite picture—her curling locks gently caressing her cheeks, her smile beaming as if God had just told her a secret, her face glowing like Moses returning from the mountaintop after an encounter with the divine. They were, I suspect, rightly concluding that I was playing out of my league. They agreed that she was, indeed, a beautiful woman.

"The thing is," I continued unreservedly, "even though all our communication has been over the internet, she still manages to do something I never thought possible: She makes me feel alive. I have energy. I am a better father, more engaged with the kids. I no longer feel like I'm just going through the motions and waiting to die. I want to be alive."

And her voice. Sometimes she would send audio messages over the internet. Her voice was the most soothing sound, warm and tender, soft and innocent. It just completely melted me. I told my parents I could have listened to her read a calculus textbook and fallen asleep at peace.

They looked at me as if the other shoe had finally dropped. They had been noticing the spring in my step, my increased focus and energy. They had noticed my own voice growing clearer, stronger, happier. They explained that they had been wondering what had gotten into me, but that they didn't dare ask for fear of making me self-conscious.

Once again, however, my dad unveiled his uncanny ability to read me. He had been peering into my soul and had seen a man blossoming before his eyes.

"We believe you have been 'dead' for quite a long time," he explained. "We have been worried about you, praying that God would be pleased to reinvigorate you in some way. And this is clearly an answer to prayer."

That led me to still more openness.

"Here's what you don't know," I said. "You may remember that last August I sent her a message telling her I would be going 'radio silent' for a while, that I would be off social media. I told her I would not be responding to her. But she kept sending me messages. She kept me up to date on the issues she was dealing with. Every day I would read her messages; they were lifelines to me."

Although I did not respond to her messages, she was able to tell that I was reading them. After seven months of my silence, she sent me a message asking how I was doing. I didn't respond. Then she had a dream. In it I sent a limousine for her; when it arrived where I was, standing behind me to greet her was an array of witnesses. The scene then changed to a romantic candlelit dinner, where I took her hands in mine, adopting a posture of love and protection. She woke crying out to God, asking Him why He would tease her in that way.

She told God—after wrestling with Him all morning—that she would send one more message; if I did not respond, then she would know the dream was not from God, and she would move on.

She sent this message: "R. C., did I say something to offend you, so that you no longer respond to me?"

Within an hour, at 12:41 P.M., for the first time in seven months, I answered her. In case they hadn't understood, I explained it to my parents now: "Like Gideon of ancient days, she put down a fleece, and God answered her with perfect clarity."

I went on to explain my plan. I was going to fly from Orlando to Indiana to visit her. If it were just a silly internet thing, we would know, and that would be that. If not, we would move forward. My parents were ecstatic for me, rejoicing with me. They encouraged me to pursue this woman who was such an encouragement to me.

As I made my way to the door to head home, my father determined that he had better be clear with his counsel.

"I have just two words for you," he said, "wisdom from your dear old dad. Are you ready?"

"Yes, sir," I said with bated breath. "What are the two words?"

"Hurry . . . Up!"

Aside from my parents' faithful call to repent and believe the gospel, this was the greatest advice I'd ever been given.

I did hurry up. I flew to Indiana earlier than I had planned to surprise her. As she waited for the elevator at her work, she sensed someone behind her, turned, saw me, and squealed, "R. C.!" She then asked what I was doing there.

And the first words she ever heard from me, face-to-face, were these: "This is me pursuing you."

By God's grace, I woke up. By God's grace, I hurried up. By God's grace, I pursued her. By God's grace, she couldn't leave me behind. By God's grace, I caught her. By God's grace, she is the deep conduit of God's grace in my life. I walked out of my own self-imposed tomb—not to the thundering voice of Jesus commanding Lazarus but to the whispering voice of Jesus, through my wife, inviting me.

By God's grace we will, tonight, as we did this morning, read together from God's Word and lift one another up before the Mercy Seat in prayer. By God's grace I will soon, as I have done with every preceding chapter, read to my greatest encourager the words of this chapter.

My father not only married my wife and me but also loved my wife and me. And this is why he gave me such sage counsel. He understood through experience what it is like to have a woman love you as you are, a woman who believes in you, a woman who inspires you, a woman whom you long to protect, to wash, to cherish, and to hold. He knew all that because he had all that in my mother. He knew what a gift it is to have a helper fit for you.

My father invested himself in me. He longed to leave my sister and me an inheritance. But he knew there were things far more valuable. He knew and embraced the wisdom of Solomon who said, "Houses and riches are an inheritance from fathers, but a prudent wife is from the LORD" (Proverbs 19:14). And I am learning daily the glorious truth that King Lemuel learned at the feet of his mother: "Who can find a virtuous wife? For her worth is far above rubies" (Proverbs 31:10).

Two Words

My father has passed on to glory. I no longer have direct access to his wisdom. He prepared me for this, however, by encouraging me to take for my bride the daughter of encouragement, the wise woman who calls out to me. I am not alone. I am a man with the greatest wife in the world. She is my one safe place, my shelter from the storm.

If you are a single man, if you have wanted to receive good counsel from R. C. Sproul, and if you know someone who is even half the woman that my dear wife is, I have some wisdom for you that I received from the lips of my father: "Hurry up!"

And give thanks and praise for His good gift.

24

Me and My Shadow

It can be an awkward thing introducing myself. Most people I meet have never heard of my father. And many of those are perfectly wonderful, godly Christians. We all tend to live in our own bubbles and think *our* world is *the* world. The evangelical world is much bigger than my little corner of it, so I ought not to be surprised when folks are unfamiliar with my name or my father's.

Other people whom I meet have a vague awareness of my father's name. You see it in their eyes, as they swiftly scroll their memory banks, trying to place the name. Some of them tell me that they've read one of my books or have heard me on Christian radio. I let them know that that's possible, but that it's far more likely it was my dad's books or radio program.

Then there are those who actually know who my dad is—and know that I am not him. The response from this crowd is usually one of three things. Some get all bug-eyed and tongue-tied; they seem to think they've been granted an audience with royalty. Of course they have. My elder Brother is King of kings after all. But then again, they are just as much royalty as I am, having the same elder Brother.

Some, however, sadly make room for the green-eyed monster: jealousy. They decide instantly that they don't like me because I was blessed with what they had long hoped for. They begin with distaste and distrust toward me, looking at me as if I somehow had cut in line to secure my parents.

Then there is an all-too-large number of folks who meet me and begin with compassion. They actually feel sorry for me that I have to carry the weight of living in the shadows, of being the son, of the famous R. C. Sproul. They assume I must feel either some unbearable burden to fill my father's oversized shoes or else some insurmountable sorrow that I have lived my life in being unfavorably compared to him.

The envious ones think I've lived my life basking in his light; the sympathetic ones, that I've been living in his shadow.

The truth is that I did not grow up in his shadow. The world in which I lived as a boy, and the world in which he lived, were fairly distinct. My school friends and their families, by and large, had no idea who my father was or what he did. Most people, even in the evangelical world, had no idea who he was as I was growing up. My father wrote books and spoke at conferences, but his following was relatively small. It was growing as I was growing, but it was still small nevertheless.

It wasn't until I had graduated college that his ministry really began to spread. But as I pursued a graduate degree at the University of Mississippi, a secular university, my world remained mostly distinct. There was some overlap, however.

My father taught each spring semester at Reformed Theological Seminary in Jackson, Mississippi. Ole Miss was just a hop, skip, and a jump up the highway. In the spring of 1989, I trekked down to Jackson to join the well-known activist Roy McMillan and his wife,

Beverly, in blocking the doors of a local abortion mill. Several dozen of us were dragged away by the local police, booked, and jailed. We were released later that day, and as we made our way out of the jail facility, a news crew approached Roy, wanting an interview. "Roy! Roy! Can we ask you a few questions?"

"Sure," Roy responded. But then he paused, turned around to find me, and said, "You do it."

Whether he wanted me on camera because I was a fresh face in an Ole Miss shirt or because I was R. C. Sproul's son, a known commodity in Jackson, I'm still not sure. Either way, I was happy to oblige.

It wasn't until I went to seminary and began working for Ligonier, my father's ministry, that my father's shadow loomed over my life. Work, school, church, my social circle—all consisted of people who knew who my father was. As I look back over my life, I think it was at this point that I turned into an introvert. I had never been the world's biggest social butterfly to begin with, but at one point I had been outgoing and not in the least bit shy.

What changed was that, in my father's shadow, every relationship I had was potentially tainted by less than honorable motives. People were generally very friendly to me. But I began to wonder why. Was it me they were interested in, or did they want to take in a bit of my father's reflected glory? Did they see me as a means to an end, as a way to get closer to my father so that they might then drop his name in casual conversation?

This was never clearer to me than those times when I was invited to church conferences. Invariably, while my host was driving me to the airport to catch my plane home, he would ask my opinion of the event. Did I think it had turned out well? Had I felt welcome? Had they treated me well? All these questions, it seemed to me, were just leading to the real question: "Do you think your dad would be interested in coming to next year's conference?"

I'm not sure who walked away from these conversations more disappointed: my host, having learned they probably weren't going to have my father at their conference, or me, wondering why I had even been invited. Sadly, this happened more often than I would like to admit.

When I have talked with "fans" of my father, I have certainly agreed with their assessments of him. Many tell me something along the lines of, "Your father has had such a profound impact on my life. His teaching has shaped who I am." To which I always reply, simply, "Me too."

I understand their appreciation because I feel it too, down to my toes. I never resented the accolades he received. He earned them, by being a faithful steward of the gifts God gave him. It was simply that I didn't like the way his accolades and recognition seemed to affect my ordinary relationships.

Although I didn't want to do so, I found myself harboring a certain level of skepticism toward others, in an effort to protect myself. It's sad, but true: When it becomes a "prize" of some sort for others to get close to you, you tend to lose interest in those friendships. And that gets lonely.

On the plus side, dealing with the impact of my father's fame on my relationships taught me to cherish the few friendships I had that I was confident were genuine. I have friends, genuine friends, for which I give thanks. Some still, to this day, do not know who my father is. Some knew me well before they knew who my father was. And some know me, and knew him, and love us for what we are, in ourselves.

My counsel to others is simple enough: Treat the people you admire the way you would like to be treated, like a normal person. Sounds simple enough, but it's remarkably true and profoundly appreciated.

A few years ago I was surprised to find Steven Tyler in a men's room at the Nashville airport. If you don't know who he is, you are already more pious than me. Tyler is the lead singer of the band Aerosmith. He was washing his hands, arranging his hair. Part of me wanted to ask him, riffing on the opening line of "Dream On," the band's first and biggest hit, "Are all those lines in your face getting clearer?" Instead, I said nothing at all. He is a man who is truly and genuinely famous (and in turn, the father of a famous daughter, the actress Liv Tyler). But he was just trying to relieve himself, and he deserved to have a moment when he could forget that he was famous. I respected that and said nothing at all.

My father was never interested in the trappings of fame. He wasn't one to seek special treatment, and you certainly would never find him asking a traffic cop or a maître d', "Do you know who I am?"

In fact, it was his habit to engage in real, personal conversations with those who tend to be looked past, those who are often seen as merely a means to an end—waiters, tellers, cashiers, and the like. (I'd also include grocery attendants, but I am pretty sure my father has been inside a grocery store fewer times than President George H. W. Bush, who was once "amazed" at grocery store scanners when he made a trip during his presidency.) All that being said, my father did realize, again, that in a certain small pond, he was famous. And he always handled that fact with such grace and charisma.

How easily he might have become jaded. How easily he might have sloughed off at fulfilling his expected duty of smiling politely when meeting yet another "fan." But that was not the kind of man he was. He was always ready to warmly greet fellow believers who shared a similar passion for the truths of God.

In fact, he consistently made it a point to find a point of contact whenever he met "fans." He would make note of their hometown or of their favorite sports teams. He would encourage them for buying classic theological books. He would sit at a book-signing table, the line snaking out of the room, and shake hands, sign books, have pictures taken (no flash please), and never fail to be kind.

I don't know exactly how he did it, but I suspect my mother had a lot to do with it. He was always comfortable with her, and he was almost always with her. My parents met in grade school. They started going steady in junior high school and were wed while he was still in college. And they had fifty-eight years together.

My mom knew him when no one knew him. My mom loved him when no one loved him. My mom believed in him when no one believed in him. She was his rock, his support, his comfort, his peace.

Like the rest of us, she too lived in his shadow. But those who truly knew them both knew well that they were one. There was no R. C. without Vesta. There was no Vesta without R. C. Luther had his Katie, and R. C. had his Vesta, the goddess of hearth and home.

My mother never gave a public talk. She never wrote a book. All she did was love and encourage my father, my sister, and me. I suspect that when you get to heaven, you will find my father there. But closer to the throne of glory, you'll find my mom.

Which is what I wish we could all remember when dealing with the power of celebrity in the Christian world. I admire many of my father's colleagues. Sinclair Ferguson is one who comes to mind. He is a great hero to me. Ravi Zacharias also inspires me. But the reason I love these men is the same reason I love my father and my mother—

because they love Jesus and because their lives bear testimony to this reality.

I'm not impressed by mere intellectual firepower. What moves me is when someone impresses upon me the glory of Christ. My father did that in spades, in all that he taught and in how he lived. My mother did the same. If Sinclair were my pastor in a tiny little church, if Ravi were my professor in an out-of-the-way little college, I would love and admire them as much as I do well-known men.

The message of the resurrected Christ Jesus is a message that is glorious. The messengers, not so much. On those occasions through the years when someone would praise a sermon I had preached, I would often respond, "I'm grateful that I get to preach a great gospel." The greatness is not in the preaching, but in the gospel.

I don't want to be looked down on out of envy for the father with whom I've been blessed. Nor do I want to be fussed over like royalty. And I certainly do not want to be a means to someone's unspoken end, or pitied for living my life in my father's shadow. Instead, I want to stand beside my father in the only safe place—in Jesus' shadow.

25

The Good Fight

One of the many classes I was privileged to take from my father in seminary was a course on homiletics. Fancy word, indeed, but it encompasses a fairly simple concept. Homiletics is the art of preaching.

While my father neither read nor wrote any books on public speaking, he was rather an expert. One of the first lessons he gave us was on the importance of losing our self-consciousness. It is hard to speak well, he constantly reminded us, when all you can think about is that you are speaking in front of a crowd. I have read polls in the past that have suggested the deepest fear of most Americans was not death or dismemberment but rather speaking in front of a crowd.

The way my father approached this basic human fear was rather unorthodox, but he assured us he had a surefire plan to help us overcome our fears. And, as was his habit, he used me as his guinea pig. He told us if we could do something silly in front of others, it would help us relax. Then he instructed me to come before the class, lie down on the floor, and act out being a piece of bacon sizzling in a pan.

If ever there were a way to remove any feeling of self-superiority, this would certainly do. I popped, herked, and jerked on the ground, acting out a piece of bacon frying, to the delight of my classmates. If that particular class was any indication of how well my father's unorthodox method worked, it worked brilliantly.

Yet for all my father's confidence behind a pulpit or in front of a microphone, and despite his abundant talent, there was one place my father lacked confidence: as father of a young man. As I grew older, he grew increasingly unsure of himself as a dad. And for a good reason. He modeled his fathering on the man he loved and admired, his own father, Robert C Sproul. But my father never got to experience being fathered beyond seventeen, his age when his father died.

Another lesson from my dad's class was his encouragement to us to read the text of Scripture existentially. He did not mean, of course, that we should come to the text armed with existential philosophy. Rather, he wanted us to remember that the Bible was true, real history, with real people, just like us. He wanted us to enter into the pathos of the men and women in the Bible. They weren't mere flannel graph cartoons designed to teach moral lessons but were flesh and blood. If you've heard my father preach on Abraham's sacrifice of Isaac, you know just what I mean. My father entered into Abraham's angst, not making it real but rather helping us to *see* that it was real.

It is not, however, just the real struggles of people in Scripture that we should be willing to enter into but our own struggles. My father's ability to be open about his own failures—his failures not as a father, but as a son; not as a speaker, but as a listener—was him at his most vulnerable.

My father, like his son, adored his father. My grandfather was, at one and the same time, larger than life while tender and close. When my father was fifteen, however, his father suffered a series of debilitating strokes, leaving him severely weakened. It was my father's duty each night to carry his father, fireman style, to the dining room table, and later, to carry him to his bed.

From time to time he spoke of the heartache he went through during that time in his life. He knew a thing or two about the dark glasses through which young men are tempted to look at the world. As daunting as it was for my father to deal with his father's illness and, a few years later, his death, none of that compared to the burden my father carried during the moment that separated my grandfather's illness from his death.

My grandfather lay on his deathbed. His strength was fading as quickly as the color on his face. Still, he wanted to leave a legacy, to punctuate a life of faithfulness in following Jesus with his own epitaph. With strained breathing, as my father stood beside him, he said the poignant words of the Apostle Paul: "I have fought the good fight, I have finished the race, I have kept the faith" (2 Timothy 4:7).

My father did not encourage his dying father in that point. He did not give his "amen" to his father's dying profession of faith. He said, instead, anger in his voice, "No. Don't say that."

Those would be the last words he would ever speak to his father.

As I heard, for the first time, my father recounting that defining moment in his life, I was consumed with both pity and resolve. Pity for my father who, because he carried this burden from his youth, was no longer invincible in my eyes. He was merely human. I could not begin to imagine the regret that followed him every day of his life. To speak words of denial to the one man he most deeply revered, and at that holy moment when his father was crossing through the veil, was beyond my comprehension.

My resolve was simple: I would learn this lesson from my father. I would not need to experience the agony he did by going through it myself. I would hold on to the wisdom his telling bestowed. And when my father was in his last hour, he would hear from his son words of encouragement. I would never forget. And at that moment when my father would go to see his earthly father in his heavenly glory, he would go with a blessing from the lips of his son.

I did not have an opportunity to have a conversation with my father in his last days. By the time I arrived at his deathbed, he was already in a coma. I have heard it said that when we are in such a condition, we have no ability to respond to others, but that we may very well be able to hear and understand what is being spoken. Embracing that hope, I took the opportunity to speak to him when it was just the two of us in the room.

> I remember, Dad, about what you said to your father when he was dying. I know what a weight that was for you to carry all these years. And I determined not to follow in those particular footsteps. But I need you to understand why. You know how much it has always meant to me to have you be proud of me. You know that I have long understood that my greatest earthly fear is that I might somehow disappoint you. I confess that a part of that is selfish. It always felt so good to me to make you proud. Every word of encouragement you ever spoke to me I treasured. But the reason I wanted, and especially now want, you to be proud of me is for your sake. I want you to be pleased with the job you did in raising me. I don't want you going to your

reward carrying the burden of feeling like you have failed me.

Because you haven't failed me. I know I have, through the years, often brought shame upon your name. I asked you to let me carry this name, and then fumbled it more than once. That's okay with me.

My point though isn't that you were ever a perfect father, and that I alone blew it. I'm not falling on my sword here, in order to ease your conscience. No, Dad. You were a great father, not because you never failed us, not because I grew up to become a model citizen of the kingdom of God. You were a great father because you did the one thing most needful for me, or for any other son. You, with all your flaws, in dealing with me and all my flaws, didn't merely encourage me to buckle down and try harder. You didn't coax and cajole. Instead, Dad, you told me about Jesus. You told me the only thing I could do about my flaws and my failures, about my cosmic treasons, my shames, and my scandals, was to run to Him. Jesus, you told me, while we were yet sinners, died for us. Jesus came into this world to save sinners, of which I am the chief. Because of Jesus, Dad, my heavenly Father is proud of me. Because of Jesus, I am His son. Because of Jesus, the Jesus that you so faithfully taught me about, I have a perfect Father who sees me as His perfect son, who loves me with a perfect love.

Because of Jesus, redeeming you, sending you His Spirit, therefore, because of you, I know Jesus.

Every one of our sins, every one of my sins, are forgiven. Our Father remembers them no more. And soon you will be like Jesus, for you will see Him as He is. He used you to give me the same hunger, the same hope. Which is why, Dad, I can say to you with the greatest of confidence, that He has fought the good fight. He has finished the race. He kept the faith. Go, and rest in Christ.

In the ensuing months after his passing, I continued to wrestle with my own shame. I wanted him to be able to go to his grave in peace, free of any worries. I wanted him to be confident that his ministry would continue on after him, in capable hands that he could trust. I wanted him to know that through his work, people around the world would continue to be awakened to the holiness of God in all its fullness.

Then I remembered what he had always told me, the central message, that there is good news: that Jesus has atoned for our sins, and that He reigns at the right hand of the Father. The first Christians confessed the most simple of creeds. What united them was this great conviction, *Christos ho Kurios*, Christ is Lord. And His kingdom is forever.

My father now has the eyes to see that he is on the true and eternal Mount Zion, the city of the living God, the heavenly Jerusalem, in an innumerable company of angels, in the general assembly and church of the firstborn who are registered in heaven, in the presence of God, the judge of all—that he is gathered there with the souls of just men made perfect (Hebrews 12:22, 23).

His ministry and work are in trusted hands because it never was his ministry and it never was in his hands. The work is ever and always the work of Jesus. It has always rested in His scarred hands. And the gates of hell will not prevail against it.

My father was just one messenger. The power and the glory was always in the message. He had feet of clay, just like you and me. But, just like us, his feet had been washed by Jesus Himself. And then those feet of clay became beautiful feet indeed as his Lord sent him forth with the good news of peace, to deliver the glad tidings of good things (Romans 10:15).

The message will continue to go forth until all of the elect are brought in from the four corners of the world. And it will not return void.

My father was quick to repeat the bit of wisdom that "Cemeteries are full of 'indispensable' men." There was room, when my father passed on to glory, for one more. The only indispensable Man walked out of His cemetery after three days, never to return there. Now He sits at the right hand of the Father, and from thence He shall come to judge the living and the dead.

Not long before my father's passing, my good wife, seeking to build me up, asked if he would be willing to write a blessing for us. He handwrote the blessing, and, for good measure, recorded it, so we could hear his voice giving it. We will cherish it the rest of our days:

Blessing for R. C. and Lisa

From the foundation of the world, from all eternity, God has known R. C. and Lisa. That knowledge was not only cognitive, but redemptive; that knowledge was a knowledge in the Son, in Christ. From the covenant of redemption to this very day,

God has known R. C. and Lisa. Indeed by His omniscient and perfect Providence, He has brought you to the holy and sacred communion of marriage. Only the Father knew the consequences of that union. Only in His mercy would He not only know but foreordain every ounce of pain and travail that would be visited upon you.

Surely the hand of His Providence has been heavy upon you. But the glorious reality is that it is His hand that is upon you. That hand carries a special mercy that is a tender mercy, a mercy that is not always immediately apparent yet is undoubtedly true. It is Hesed, a Loyal Love, a covenant fidelity that is unmatched by any human endeavor.

His vocation remains intact—His call to service is unabated and undiminished. Any blessing I can offer you pales into insignificance in the light of His blessing and calling to you, a calling that is without repentance and sure.

I don't know the outcome of your Providential future, but I know, and you know, the One who does, the One who does all things well.

You have my fullest blessing, but more important, His, which reaches to eternity. You have My love, and Mom's forever,

Amen.

I miss my father, and I look forward to that glorious day when I will be reunited with him in glory. But for now, I cling to the One who redeemed us both. I am at peace, because I belong, body and soul, in life and in death, to the Prince of Peace.

Afterword

I did not grow up as, or with, R. C., but I was blessed to have a brief time to converse with R. C. the elder (or as my husband liked to call him, "R. C. the Less Handsome"). Two things immediately struck me then that shine through here: He was an open man with me, and he dearly loved his son. These came together one morning when he said to me over the breakfast table, "My son has been dead a long time . . . and never have I seen him more alive, since you came into his life. He has told us of your fervent prayers and the fleece you had laid before God, and we are thankful for you, Dear One." He was referring to a season that I had prayed fervently for R. C., literally 10 to 12 hours a day for 14 days, while fasting. I was seeking God regarding this man.

As I travailed in fervent prayer, God impressed on me several truths. R. C. was a man wrapped in grave clothes, resigned to die, swallowed up in defeat and beset by the ills of this fallen world. My prayer for R. C. was simply this: "Oh God, let him live. Oh God, let him breathe." Over and over and over, day after day, I cried out for God to give him life, to prophecy to his dry bones and to say to him in comfort and hope, "You will live and not die."

If you are an intercessor you understand the challenge. After the fourteenth day I felt released to know that God was bringing this man forth. God heard my prayers, even as He heard the prayers of R. C.'s parents. We all witnessed a dead man come to life.

The truth is, this shouldn't surprise us—that's precisely what God does. R. C. Sr. was always quick to remind us all that not only did Jesus make it *possible* for us to have eternal life, but He calls us to life. He didn't invite or entice Lazarus to walk out of his tomb, but commanded it—"Lazarus, come out!" (John 11:43).

R. C. Jr. told me that I was for him the voice of Jesus calling him from the grave. I know I was blessed and chosen to witness the miracle. Like Lazarus, R. C. has stumbled plenty as the grave clothes have come off. But he, like his father before him, keeps returning to the gospel. He keeps pointing us both back that all-important source.

Although my years with R. C. Sr. were too short, we both understood that it is God who established us before all time. It is He that ordains every one of our days before one of them ever came to be. He refines us continually, conforming us to His image. Every assigned trial, every stretching hardship, every turbulent tribulation is creating in us character to persevere, to stand and proclaim a Holy God and His message that proclaims liberty and sets the captive free. In the midst of some of our most difficult challenges after my husband's DUI, we relocated back to my home in Indiana. His health challenges ensued for ten months of our first year together. God was our anchor, our refuge, our high tower then, just as He is now and forever more. In the midst of our weighty, ongoing trials and tribulations, my father-in-law called me one afternoon, asking me how he could be of help. Without hesitation I asked, "Would you speak a blessing over us?"

Of all the things I could ask, why would I have chosen the spoken blessing? It seems like a practice reserved exclusively for Old Testament times, does it not? Yet I did so for four reasons:

- *A blessing protects.* "The LORD bless thee, and keep thee" (Numbers 6:24, KJV).

- *A blessing imparts grace.* "The LORD make His face shine upon thee, and be gracious unto thee" (Numbers 6:25, KJV).
- *A blessing imparts peace.* "The LORD lift up His countenance upon thee, and give thee peace" (Numbers 6:26, KJV).
- *A blessing requires faith.* "He staggered not at the promise of God through unbelief; but was strong in faith, giving glory to God; and being fully persuaded that, what He had promised, He was able also to perform" (Romans 4:20–21, KJV).

Speaking the Word of God over your family is one of the most powerful forces for imparting truth, vision, and the power of God's grace. Your tongue can be used to impart life by speaking a blessing or to impart death by speaking a curse. We remind ourselves of how God sees a person when we use Scripture to impart a blessing. "The blessing of the LORD makes one rich, and He adds no sorrow with it" (Proverbs 10:22).

R. C. Sr. knew God's hand had been heavy upon us, but he wanted us to see that it was indeed God's hand that was upon us. We had a covenant love established from all time—*hesed*, a loyal love.

R. C. Sr. has gone on ahead of us to His reward—that is, the reward that Jesus earned, not what we have earned—but his message and his blessing over us continues to bear fruit. Even in our family, we have children at home under our care. And they are being told the same glorious message—Jesus came into this world to save sinners. By His life, death, resurrection, and ascension, we are redeemed, loved, adopted, and secured. We are passing on the message, the legacy of legacies. We are instructing our children that they must believe and likewise instruct their children to rest solely in the finished work of Jesus. By His grace R. C. and I are together, laboring to fight the good fight, to finish the race, and to keep the faith—knowing our Savior will lose none of His, but will raise us up on the last day (John 6:44).

Lisa C. Sproul

Notes

1 William Hale, *The Autobiography & Deliverance of Mark Rutherford* (New York: Dodd, Mead & Company, 1899), 11.

2 Martin Luther, *Letters of Spiritual Counsel*, trans. and ed. Theodore G. Tappert (Vancouver, British Columbia: Regent College 2003), 86–87.

3 John Piper, "Unashamed Allegiance: My Tribute to R.C. Sproul (1939–2017)." DesiringGod. December 14, 2017. https://www.desiringgod.org/articles/unashamed-allegiance.

4 C. S. Lewis, *The Abolition of Man* (New York: HarperOne, 1996), 67.

5 C. S. Lewis, *The Weight of Glory* (New York: HarperOne, 2001) 45–46.

6 R. T. Kendall, *The Power of Humility: Living Like Jesus* (Lake Mary: Charisma House, 2011), 118–19.

7 G. K. Chesterton, *Orthodoxy* (New York: John Lane Company, 1908), 56.

CPSIA information can be obtained
at www.ICGtesting.com
Printed in the USA
BVHW040638090519
R9905100001B/R99051PG547432BVX1B/1/9